#56c00
3/14/11

UNEQUAL FORTUNES

FORTUNES

Snapshots from the
South Bronx

UNEQUAL FORTUNES

Snapshots from the South Bronx

ARTHUR LEVINE
LAURA SCHEIBER

Teachers College, Columbia University
New York and London

Published by Teachers College Press, 1234 Amsterdam Avenue, New York, NY 10027

Library of Congress Cataloging-in-Publication Data

Levine, Arthur.
  Unequal fortunes : snapshots from the South Bronx / Arthur Levine, Laura Scheiber.
     p. cm.
  Includes bibliographical references.
  ISBN 978-0-8077-5075-9 (pbk.)—ISBN 978-0-8077-5076-6 (hardcover)
  1. Education, Urban—New York (State)—New York. 2. People with social disabilities—New York (State)—New York. 3. Levine, Arthur—Anecdotes. 4. Bronx (New York, N.Y.)—Biography—Anecdotes. I. Scheiber, Laura. II. Title.
  LC5133.N4L48 2010
  370.9747'275—dc22

                                                                    2010013815

ISBN 978-0-8077-5075-9 (paper)
ISBN 978-0-8077-5076-6 (hardcover)

Printed on acid-free paper
Manufactured in the United States of America

17   16   15   14   13   12   11   10   8   7   6   5   4   3   2   1

This Book is Dedicated to Our Friend,
Leonel Disla

Contents

PART III: WHAT CHANGED?

PART IV: REVIVING THE AMERICAN DREAM

Preface

THIS IS THE STORY of two boys growing up on the same street in the Bronx 40 years apart. Arthur left to go to college, and Leonel (Leo) was murdered. More than an account of two lives, this book is a testament to the loss of opportunity and the death of the American dream on that street and across urban America.

As a counterpoint, this book examines the lives of two other youngsters on that street today, Juan Carlos and Carlos, who are educationally successful. We identify the lessons that can be learned from their experiences and discuss what will be necessary to revive the American dream for all youngsters across this country.

The research and writing of this book was an emotional rollercoaster for us. The high points were extraordinary.

Arthur got to go back in time, to reconnect with the neighborhood where he grew up, thought of as home, and left 30 years earlier. It was a world he thought available to him only in memories that were growing hazy. He got to revisit the apartment where he and his family lived (now the home of Carlos and his family), the school he attended, the streets on which he played, the synagogue where he went to Hebrew school and had his Bar Mitzvah, and the stores where he shopped. He had a chance to view today's neighborhood through the window of his childhood bedroom.

We brought back Arthur's childhood friends who grew up on the same block in order to share memories, visit the places that stood out in their lives, to play a last game of punch ball, and to meet the current residents of the neighborhood.

We met the wonderful people who live in the neighborhood today. They embraced us and invited us into their lives. Laura became almost a family member replete with an extended family of grandparents, mothers and fathers, uncles, aunts, cousins, brothers and sisters, and later their children in the neighborhood and the Dominican Republic.

We watched with wonder and joy as two young men who weren't sure they would complete high school in a neighborhood where dropping out was the norm, earned high school diplomas and attended college, where they are about to graduate.

The lows were gut wrenching. We cried and continue to grieve over a vibrant, 19-year-old, who had become a friend and the focus of this book, who was shot and killed by the police. One night, he just disappeared from our lives in a horrible and violent way, leaving his family, friends, and us disbelieving and devastated.

Getting to know the neighborhood again for Arthur and for the first time for Laura was extraordinarily painful. The grinding effects of poverty and the lack of opportunity for the children and their families was heart wrenching and made us angry. For Arthur, this was compounded by remembering a neighborhood in which the American Dream had once flourished.

Writing this book was a chance to repay a debt to all the people who welcomed us into their lives; to tell the story of a friend, who, like too many youngsters in his neighborhood, died far too soon; to salve the increasing pain we felt as the research progressed; and to plead to the people of this nation to save the children in this neighborhood and in poor inner cities across this country. The most important part of this story is that this nation knows how to do this. It makes moral and economic sense. All that is needed is the will to do it.

Acknowledgments

THIS BOOK WOULD NOT have been possible without the help of many, many people.[1] First and foremost, we are enormously grateful to Leonel Disla, Juan Carlos Reyes, and Carlos Pilarte, who spent hundreds of hours talking to us, writing journal entries, including us in their day-to-day lives, inviting us to important events, and putting up with our never-ending questions. This book is the result of their hard work, dedication, and generosity. We are thankful for their friendships and for all that they have taught us.

We are also grateful to Arthur's childhood friends Barry Bernstein, Debby Fleishner, and Jim Welber for meeting with us for interviews, engaging in countless phone calls, attending group meetings in person and on the telephone, participating in briefings and debriefings, and giving two full weekends to meet with Leo and his friends. Above all, we thank them for caring so much about the boys and for nagging us to complete the book.

Leo's immediate family was beyond generous to us. Leo's mom Miriam Disla, brother Lisandro Disla, sister Iliana (Maholi) Disla, and in later years uncle Juan (Siso) welcomed us into their home as if we were family and spent endless hours patiently and warmly answering questions about their lives while serving refreshments. For several years, Lisandro was just as involved in the project as Leo, Juan Carlos, and Carlos. He met with us for interviews, helped transcribe, and actively participated in the weekend gatherings with Arthur and his childhood friends. When Laura went to the Dominican Republic and stayed with Leo's family, Leo's grandma, Teresa, acted as a surrogate grandparent. Leo's father, "Moreno" and the entire extended family—including uncles Radhame and Nelson, aunt Francisca, and cousins

Placido (Ruddy), Maria Luisa (Rosemary), Willy, and Dayra—treated her like royalty. Their neighborhood friends also pitched in. When Laura got sick and had to go the hospital, they took turns visiting her for 48 hours straight.

We don't really have the words to thank Carlos's family adequately. Imagine a total stranger showing up at your door step, asking not only to come in uninvited, but also to hang out with your family for a decade to find out what your life is like. That's what this family did. From that first encounter, Carlos's father Isamel Pilarte, mother Milagros Pilarte, sisters Luz and Jaqueline, brothers Ismael and Leonel, brother-in-laws Eduardo and Nelson, nieces Pamela, Jenesis, and Chantel, nephews Julio and Estevan, and cousins always made us feel at home. A "quick" visit to answer a few questions, generally turned into a 2- or 3-hour event, in which we were always offered food and Dominican tea (which Laura swears is the best tea she has ever tasted). They were just as generous with their time. Ismael, who usually had one day off of work a week, never complained about talking for hours about his life in the Dominican Republic and the Bronx and his experience in raising his son Carlos. Carlos's mom, who usually did not feel well due to Parkinson's disease and high blood pressure, was usually more concerned about whether her guest felt comfortable in their home than attending to her own discomforts. When Carlos's parents were not home, Carlos's sisters, brothers, nephews and nieces always extended the same hospitality as their parents. Laura first visited the Dominican Republic in 2001 and stayed with Carlos's family. We have learned that Dominican hospitality is something that cannot be described but simply experienced.

Laura also spent a good amount of time with Juan Carlos's family. Juan Carlos's mom Florinda, his stepfather Alejandro, his brother Richard, and his sister Ivelisse (Ive) treated Laura more like an extended family member than a researcher. She was invited to family events and was always offered a meal. Like the other families, we are extremely grateful for their patience in answering our many interview questions.

While all the neighborhood friends of Leo, Carlos, Juan Carlos, and Lisandro were always respectful and helpful, several people deserve special attention. During the 10 years of research, no one was more open and honest with us than Ana Lopez, Leo's former girlfriend. Lisandro's ex-girlfriend Betty also made herself very available to us, inviting us to family celebrations like their daughter's first birthday party. We are also thankful to Jose, who started with us on this project, but could no longer participate when he moved away from the neighborhood. To all the friends—inlcuding former and current girlfriends, Venus and Jakiris—who let us into your worlds, we thank you.

We also owe a debt of gratitude to several of the school people in the lives of Leo, Juan Carlos, and Carlos. A very special thank you goes to Leo's basketball coach, his eighth-grade guidance counselor, his high school attendance officer, and his Job Corps counselor. We are very thankful to the former principals of PS 79 and 279 and members of their staff, who spoke with us candidly about the challenges and rewards of working at their schools. While there were many educators who helped us, we are particularly grateful to Ms. Ochoa, Ms. Mc-Guyor, Ms. Perez, and Mr. Abadia.

Peter Dillon, now superintendent of the Berkshire Hills Regional School District, but principal of New York City's Heritage School at the time of our study, is a hero in this volume. He gave Juan Carlos a third chance to succeed by admitting him to the Heritage School, looked after him with discipline and care after he enrolled, gave him the support necessary to graduate and attend college, and assembled a superb faculty to educate him, including Ms. Dhakkar, Sensei Rachel "Rocky" Rivera, Mr. Saltz, and Mr. Nichols. Plus, in the course of writing this book, he answered a gazillion questions for us.

We want to thank those people who granted us interviews while carrying out background research on the old neighborhood, including Dan Rosa, Pat Daddino, and Joseph Bodak. Dan Rosa shared with us his priceless pictures of Burnside Avenue, which are rare historical documents. We are grateful to the entire Bodak management team who made this book possible by introducing us to the family living in Arthur's old apartment.

People at Teachers College gave us logistical and emotional support throughout this project. Jacquie Spano, executive assistant to the president, was a rock. There is probably no aspect of this study in which she was not involved, including the care and feeding of the authors. More important, we are thankful to her for being a good friend and going to Leo's funeral to offer emotional support during an incredibly painful time. We are thankful to Scott Fahey who read numerous versions of this book. His humor and insight are always appreciated. We are also grateful to Alisa Lawrence, who made sure Juan Carlos, Carlos, and Leo always felt at home at the college while visiting a world very foreign to theirs. We are thankful for the work of Rocio Rivas-Jongsomjit, Analia Arevalo, Nancy Cotham Black, and the Teachers College transcription services, who helped with the tedious but much needed task of transcribing interviews.

As this book went through permutation after permutation, Joan Benham stood by us as our editor. She asked us hard questions about what we wanted to accomplish and marvelously helped us see our shortcomings. Joan is a superb editor, and we were thrilled to have the opportunity to work with her. Every aspect of this book is better, some dramatically so, because of her efforts.

The authors are grateful to Carole Saltz and her colleagues at Teachers College Press, particularly Emily Ballengee, Adee Braun, Nancy Power, Beverly Rivero, Leyli Shayegan, and Lori Tate for believing in this project and helping to turn it from an idea into a book.

We also thank the Lumina Foundation, which inadvertently spurred this book in supporting a study by Arthur and Diane Dean of college student attitudes, values, and experiences, which would include a chapter on missing persons, people who should be in college but are not. That chapter turned into this book.

There is no gift as valuable as the love and support of family and friends. We are forever grateful to our family and friends who supported our work, even when it meant cutting into family time. Arthur is grateful to his wife Linda Fentiman, who in the course of this project celebrated their 25th through 35th wedding anniversaries with him. She was kind, loving, generous and supportive throughout, even though the research and writing intruded on a number of family events. She read and commented on many, many drafts and talked through the project with Arthur too many times to count. A law professor, she helped Leo's family after his death. His daughters, Jamie and Rachel, were wonderful, serving as motivators, sounding boards and willingly accepting distractions during family vacations, particularly while finishing the writing of this volume. His sister, Thea Farhadian, helped him remember life growing up on Creston Avenue as he wrote the personal sections of the book. Her memory and her spelling were a lot better than his, even though he is the older brother. He thanks his cousins Eva, Sharon, and Barbara for reminiscing and laughing with him about their experiences growing up together.

James Fraser and Beverly Sanford of the Woodrow Wilson Foundation were counselors, critics, and friends. Carolyne Marrow handled all the logistical arrangements so as to make them seamless.

Laura is thankful to her friends who believed in this project from the beginning, particularly Crystine Goldberg, John Hanusz, Laura Catignani, Molly Chanoff, and Stephanie Trager. Shirli Michalevicz not only provided the support of a good friend, but also her wizard storyboarding and editing expertise. A special thanks goes to Laura's dear friend and former roommate, Kevin Indoe, who always welcomed Carlos, Leo, and Juan Carlos into his home when Laura conducted interviews there. Laura is also grateful to him for attending Leo's funeral with her and helping her cope during the aftermath of his death. Maria Mercurio played a critical role in helping Laura through the grieving process. Laura does not have words to express the gratitude she feels for her mom and dad, Stephen Scheiber and MaryAnn Scheiber, who always make her feel like the most accomplished person on earth, believing in her no matter what. She simply couldn't ask for better parents. She is also grateful for her brother and sister, Martin Scheiber and Lisa Haith for rooting for her on the sidelines. And finally, Laura's husband, Matthew James Harris, played the roles of life partner, friend, cheerleader, and editor. He offered her a strong shoulder to lean on through the ups and painful downs of this project. Without Matt's unconditional support, the book would not have happened.

UNEQUAL FORTUNES

FORTUNES

Snapshots from the
South Bronx

Prologue

THIS BOOK BEGAN when Arthur Levine became president of Teachers College in 1994, returning to the city where he grew up, but left nearly 30 years before to go to college. He wanted to visit his old neighborhood on Creston Avenue in the Bronx. It felt more like home than any place he had ever lived.

At first, Arthur just wanted to see his old apartment. So he knocked on the door and was turned away. The tenants had no idea who he was. His Spanish is terrible, so they couldn't understand what he said. And being an Anglo in a suit and tie, he looked like trouble.

A few years later, he tried again. This time he sent Laura, his research assistant, who was fluent in Spanish. When Laura knocked, she was accompanied by the superintendent and managing agent of the building—two people whom the family knew and trusted. She was invited to come in and arranged a visit for Arthur. When he did visit, he found the apartment much smaller and its long hallway much shorter than he remembered, which was not all that surprising since everything he revisits from his childhood seems to have shrunk with the passing years. He gushed to the residents about his memories of each of the rooms. He looked into the kitchen; nothing was where he remembered it being. He inspected the living room and found that the wall his mother had installed was still there. Poking his head into what had been his sister's room, he found it was now the property of another little girl. He checked out the bathroom and wanted to look in the closets, but couldn't think of a polite way to do that. At the end of the hall was his bedroom.

That's where we (the authors) met Carlos, who lived in Arthur's room. He was 14 years old, 5 feet 9 inches tall, dark-skinned with eyes slanted up like Sammy Sosa's and a little overweight. Born in the Dominican Republic, Carlos, a middle school student, was a sweet kid.

Carlos was the same age as Arthur when he lived there. His bed was in exactly the same place as Arthur's. His dresser was placed where Arthur's had been. When Carlos woke up in the morning, he looked out the same window Arthur did and saw the same things Arthur did at that age. Carlos brushed his teeth in the same bathroom Arthur did. Carlos ate his meals in the same kitchen where Arthur ate, and watched TV in the same living room with the furniture arranged in exactly the same way.

Carlos asked Arthur a barrage of questions about what the neighborhood was like when he lived there. We asked him the same things about the present. This conversation continued through Carlos's years in middle school, high school, and college, where he is now.

We were fascinated by our encounter with Carlos. Before going to Arthur's old apartment, we had perused the census data on the block, prepared a history of the apartment building and neighborhood, and read a bookshelf worth of publications on the South Bronx. We wandered around the neighborhood, walked into the stores, and visited the schools and churches. What this meant was that we were like tourists who read the guide book. Carlos offered us something entirely different—an opportunity to see the old neighborhood 40 years later—from Arthur's own bedroom window and through the eyes of a boy who was his age when he lived in the apartment.

We met Carlos's family living in the Creston Avenue apartment—father, mother, and niece. His mom and dad, Spanish speakers, each had 8 years of formal education. His dad was a factory worker in New Jersey, and his mom, who had worked in the same factory, was out of work owing to Parkinson's disease. With Laura's help as translator, they all agreed to participate in a study of Carlos's world.

Carlos introduced us to his two best friends—Juan Carlos and Leo. Like Carlos, both boys, aged 15, were born in the Dominican Republic. They were very sharp dressers wearing brand-name clothes—jerseys and t-shirts, baggy pants, and sneakers. Leo was tall, almost 6 feet with well-tended braids, and Juan Carlos was half a foot shorter with hair barbered weekly. Both, gang members, disliked school, finding it boring. Leo had been left back in eighth grade and Juan Carlos had been expelled from high school for hitting a security guard.

Neither of Juan Carlos's parents had completed high school. Leo's mother had more education, having completed a postsecondary teacher education program in the Dominican Republic, and his father had less, a few years of elementary school. He acquired and sold motorcycles for a living, and Leo's mother worked variously as a factory worker, cook at McDonald's, and a bathroom cleaner at Kennedy airport.

Leo, Juan Carlos, and their families agreed to join the project, and for 5 years Carlos, Juan Carlos, and Leo kept diaries of their daily lives.[1]

* * *

We had embarked on what would become a much longer project than we ever imagined, a decade long collaboration. It came to include not only Carlos's friends and extended family, but their families and friends and the institutions that touched their lives too. A part-time assignment turned into a full-time job for Laura, taking her to courts, doctors' offices, police departments, schools, colleges, clubs, parties, open school nights, stores, homes, government agencies, restaurants, funerals, and a host of other locales in the United States and the Dominican Republic. In addition to being an observer, Laura became a big sister, daughter, counselor, facilitator, and ombudsperson for Carlos, friends, and families. She was a constant presence in their lives with the exception of several months abroad.

Arthur was less intimately involved. He met with Carlos and his friends, visited their families, talked with teachers and principals, went to an occasional restaurant with the boys, attended a funeral, and invited the boys to his home and workplace many times. He also introduced the boys to several of the friends he had grown up with—Barry Bernstein, Debby Fleischner, and Jim Welber.

This book evolved substantially over time as we considered and reconsidered how best to tell the story of the decline of America's inner cities, the impact of poverty on the nation's children, and the prospects for renewal via an account of life on Creston Avenue.

Initially, we planned to write a book about Arthur's and Carlos's worlds, a comparison of the life and times of two boys who lived in the same bedroom. However, Leo was shot and killed by a police officer in 2005. We concluded that his story best demonstrated the realities of life on Creston Avenue today. Plus, of the three boys, he had written the most extensive and insightful diary.

We thought publishing Leo's diaries—which were powerful, rich and deeply moving—might be more valuable than writing a book about him. However, Leo's first and preferred language was Spanish. His English grammar was weak and his spelling was phonetic. His diary was difficult to read.

Finally, this became a book about all three boys and Arthur. It would tell the stories of Arthur and Leo, a comparison of the lives of two boys who grew up on the same street in dramatically different worlds, and had profoundly different futures. But we would also tell the stories of Carlos and Juan Carlos as a counterpoint. They are anomalies in their neighborhood. Both boys graduated from high school and went to college. Their stories demonstrate the factors that led to the educational success that eluded nearly all of their friends. Their stories also tell much about how our nation can save the millions of children like Leo, who live in our inner cities today.

* * *

This book is divided into four parts. Arthur's and Leo's stories in Parts I and II, respectively, are not written as biographical portraits, but rather as a series of vignettes, or snapshots, about the most important people and institutions in their lives—their families, friends, neighborhoods, and educations. We believe that this approach gives the reader a deeper and richer understanding of the two boys' lives, the worlds in which they grew up and the factors that influenced their futures. In our narrative, we decided to write in the third person in order to provide continuity in Arthur and Leo's stories. The names of several individuals have been changed in this book at their request, though not their stories.

The tone or voice of the stories of Arthur and Leo are different in ways that were unavoidable. Arthur's story might be described as historical writing, and Leo's, as reporting. The account of Arthur's life is a reconstruction of events that occurred a half century ago, aided and tested by conversations with his sister, childhood friends, and cousins. His parents, grandparents, aunts, uncles, and neighbors were dead at the time we began this study. A diary Arthur wrote for 5 months when he was 12 turned up in the course of the writing, but his reflections would not be confused with Anne Frank's in providing a rich portrait of family, surroundings, and life. His diary, generally a few sentences in length per day, was little more than the self-absorbed datebook of a seventh grader. Each chapter in Arthur's story begins with quotes from that diary.

The account of Leo's life is more detailed and immediate. Its descriptions are richer because they rely upon conversations, reflections, and events as they occurred, which was possible because the study was based on a decade of observation, interviews with the participants, and detailed diary writing. These accounts also touch on intimate aspects of Leo's life growing up on Creston Avenue, which were not part of

Arthur's life, such as sex, drugs, and street violence. The result is an intimate account of two lives, one of which is observed through a telescope and the other through a microscope.

The third part of this book highlights the differences in the two boys' stories. It begins with an account of a 2-day conversation among three people who grew up with Arthur and the boys, as they attempted to discover the commonalities and differences in their experiences on Creston Avenue.

The final part tells the stories of Juan Carlos and Carlos, discusses why they were successful educationally, and examines the implications of their stories for helping more low-income children get to college. We close the book with a description of the work of three organizations—I Have a Dream, the Harlem Children's Zone, and Say Yes to Education—which are attempting to apply the lessons learned from the lives of young people like Carlos and Juan Carlos to classrooms, schools, and communities. These programs demonstrate how a compassionate nation can extend the American dream to its most vulnerable children and bring hope and promise to the lives of young people who have little of either today.

* * *

In closing, we offer a caution and an admission of our biases. The caution is that it would be a mistake to read this volume as an account of the differences between growing up in a Jewish versus a Dominican community. There are four reasons.

First, this is a book about the lives of two boys. While their stories reflect the realities of living on Creston Avenue at particular moments in history, the snapshots offered in this book are of individuals—their families, friends and experiences—rather than portraits of everyone living in the neighborhood.

The second is somewhat the reverse of the first. Although Arthur and his family are Jewish, his upward mobility through education was experienced by the Catholics and Protestants in his neighborhood as well. Similarly, even though Leo was Dominican, his neighborhood included a diversity of religious and ethnic groups, all of whom were denied the opportunity Arthur and his friends experienced 40 years earlier. There is an important exception here. In Arthur's day, Blacks and Puerto Ricans in the neighborhood generally were not afforded the same opportunities as Whites. If Leo had lived there then, discrimination would likely have diminished the opportunities available to him as well.

Third, this is a book about social class and the loss of the American Dream for the poor, regardless of religion or ethnicity. Working class families 4 decades ago had access to resources: people like teachers and professionals who lived in the neighborhood and served as models and aids in promoting educational mobility, jobs that paid enough to support a family, and effective social institutions—schools, police, courts, and healthcare—that enabled children and families to pursue the American Dream. Today, the poor are isolated and concentrated. Middle-class flight and fair housing laws have resulted in the loss of economic diversity in the neighborhood. Jobs paying adequate salaries to individuals without a high school diploma have largely disappeared. Social institutions no longer serve neighborhood residents—the educational, criminal justice and health care systems are failing them.

Fourth, this is a book about changing times and the ways in which the bar for mobility has been profoundly raised. In the more than 40 years since Arthur left Creston Avenue, the United States has shifted from an industrial to an information economy. Not only has this meant the loss of industrial jobs requiring a high school diploma or less, but the fastest-growing jobs, outside the low-wage service industry, paying salaries sufficient to support a family, require more education and the highest levels of skills and knowledge in history. More than ever before, mobility and education are inextricably intertwined with a recognition that mobility requires more education than ever before. On top of this, in the current economy with the loss and relocation of jobs, even with education, mobility is severely curtailed, making it far more difficult to escape poverty.

And now our biases: We believe that education is still the foremost path out of poverty for the poor in America today. We believe this is not simply a matter of good schools, but also overcoming the barriers to education including inadequate housing, bad jobs, poor healthcare, racism, and violence, among others. We believe in the American Dream and its promise of opportunity for all Americans. We believe the American Dream has diminished as a prospect for many Americans, particularly the poor. We believe the Dream can and must be restored for all Americans and the nation has the tools to accomplish this.

PART I

ARTHUR'S STORY

1

Arthur's Family

Arthur with his parents in the South Bronx

My wish came true. I saw Cinderfella [a movie]. Tonight I went [with friend Johnny]. . . .Then we had pizza, but I am not to tell my father.

February 18, 1961

Today is my pretty sisters birthday She is qute. I love her I was a cheap louse I didn't buy her anything, but I will make it up. I didn't go to the party, but I did have cake . . .

March 2, 1961

My father is bullheaded. Today is Passover and I have to go to bed. I have
no temperature I was over heated, but he said to bed.
March 31, 1961, Arthur's seventh grade diary

ARTHUR'S FAMILY moved to Creston Avenue right after his ninth
birthday in 1957. They came from deep in the South Bronx, an
area that U.S. Presidents visited regularly in the years to come
to showcase the blight of urban America. By the time the Levine family
moved, the quality of housing was deteriorating and crime was soaring.
The local police station was nicknamed "Fort Apache," a reference
to the 19th-century wild west cavalry post surrounded by hostile In-
dians. The streets were filthy, the rodent population multiplied, and
gangs fought for control of the neighborhood. Arthur remembers an
older boy, Johnny Guzman, who was very kind to him, being gunned to
death. He remembers one night looking at a soda shop next door to his
apartment building and seeing rats eating the potato chips in the window. Whites moved out of the neighborhood and were replaced largely
by poor Puerto Ricans.

Creston Avenue was not the Levines' first choice for a new place to
live. They looked for months to find something they could afford and
finally were forced to rent an apartment more expensive than fit their
budget. They had hoped to find a place in the public housing projects,
but the waiting list was too long, and they were not called until after
they moved.

Their new neighborhood was White and working class. Ninety-
eight percent of the population was Caucasian. A little more than a
third (36%) were foreign born, overwhelmingly Eastern European,
many from Poland and Russia. The median family income in 1960 was
$6,265 or $29,633 in current dollars, 74% of the national average.

Their new home, 2078 Creston Avenue, seemed magnificent compared to the fourth-floor walk up they had left. It was actually two
apartment buildings, 2078 and 2076, joined by a common lobby with
benches, where children played on rainy days. Framing the entrance to
the buildings was a pillared concrete gate that kids rode like a horse. It
led into a small courtyard with an imposing stairway into the building
at its end and apartments on both sides of the stairway in the courtyard.

The Levines' apartment, B-3 on the first floor, seemed grand, still
smelling of fresh paint. It was what is called a classic five-room prewar
apartment. The spine was, what seemed to a young boy, an endless
hallway. Off to the right, immediately after entering the apartment,

was a kitchen, large enough to accommodate a table for six, where the family ate its meals. To the left was a room intended to serve as a dining room, but the Levines needed another bedroom more; this became Arthur's parents' bedroom. French doors in the bedroom led into a living room. Arthur's mother had the French doors covered with a wall because Arthur had badly cut his arm on the panes of a French door 2 years earlier, and perhaps too, because she wanted a modicum of privacy. Further up the hallway were two bedrooms for the children, Arthur and his young sister, Thea, with a bathroom in between the rooms.

*   *   *

Arthur's father, Meyer, called Mike, was 40 years old when the family moved. The fifth of six children of Russian shtetl immigrants, fleeing the Czar's army and Russia's pogroms, he was born the year before the United States entered World War I and grew up during the Depression. Though Mike was born in the United States, Yiddish was his first language. He didn't learn English until he started school, where he got as far as 10th grade. Mike was badly wounded during World War II, and after he returned home, he took a job in the post office because the civil service position offered security, a very appealing prospect for the Depression generation. There he worked for 4 decades, principally as a clerk, sorting letters, in New York City's main post office in Manhattan. It was dreary work that he hated. For several years, Mike worked two jobs, his day job at the post office and a night job doing security work at a bank, in order to save for a big party for Arthur's Bar Mitzvah. Several times, his dad took the test for clerk foreman—the next job up the postal career ladder—which involved weeks of study late into the night every night at the kitchen table, but he was never promoted.

Like all of us, Mike was a complex person. He loved parties, bar mitzvahs, traditional celebrations like Thanksgiving and Passover, and going to Las Vegas. His toast was always the same—"only good things"—but he was often angry, disappointed, and unhappy. To him, there was nothing more important than family. His nieces and nephews adored him, but his immediate family was afraid of him.

Arthur's dad was fiercely independent and declined help from his wife's wealthier relatives—a better job in their factory or assistance with a mortgage for a suburban house. He was proud and did not want handouts. He saw the world in black and white. Above all, what he demanded was respect. To Mike, infringement of the rules he set—getting a phone call during dinner or coming home even a few minutes late—were not indiscretions, but overt acts of disrespect. Mike raged and screamed, and then withdrew into a stony silence for days, weeks, or longer as he grew unhappier, yet he never spanked his children.

One night, Arthur and his dad were watching television, the principal form of family entertainment. There was only one TV, a console, in most of the neighborhood homes, which meant the kids and parents had to watch the same programs. On this particular evening, the television reception became fuzzy and the picture began to roll. To fix this, Arthur moved the antennae and turned the vertical control knob, which televisions had in those days. Reception got worse. His father told him to leave it alone, but Arthur thought he could fix it. The television went black; the lights in the apartment went off as did lights across the neighborhood. Arthur's father yelled, look at what you did. It was, in fact, the New York power failure of 1965. Thea still jokes that her brother was responsible.

Although Arthur loved his dad, during much of his adolescence, he was scared of him. So he tried not to ask him for anything face to face. Instead, particularly when his dad was working two jobs, Arthur would wait until he or his Dad was going to bed and leave him notes on the kitchen table asking for money to go bowling or to play miniature golf. His father always left the money, even if he was not talking to Arthur. In the morning, there would be the $2 on the kitchen table, but never a note.

His father was parsimonious at home. He sat in the dark rather than turn on a light. He walked for miles rather than pay for a bus. He would shop for hours and hours to save a few cents on a purchase of canned goods. After the sports section of the *Daily News*, he would turn to the coupons. He clocked family member phone calls and told them to get off the line after 3 minutes. During Arthur's teenage years, when the phone needed to be surgically removed from his ear, his mother hid the telephone bills from his dad. Mike was forever shutting off lights in his apartment and asking those who left them on whether they owned stock in the electric company.

But Mike—who wanted to put on a big spread for any event he hosted, particularly Arthur's Bar Mitzvah—fought to pay the check whenever he was out with others. He advised Arthur that when you are at a bar, particularly with non-Jews, make sure you pay for the first round. People should never think you are a cheap Jew. What made this especially memorable advice was that Mike rarely drank.

For New Year's Eve, he would bring a kitchen chair to the hallway closet, reach into the top shelf, pull down several bottles of liquor, only the best brands, and pour everyone drinks. People rarely if ever actually had a second drink despite his father's encouragement. "Come on;

how about another?" The exceptions were an aunt and uncle who once or twice accepted the invitation and were referred to thereafter behind their backs as the *shikas* (Yiddish for drunks). People just didn't drink in Arthur's family. When Arthur met his future wife's family for the first time and found out they had a drink with dinner every evening, he was shocked, fearing he was entering the film *Days of Wine and Roses.*

When he and Linda Fentiman got married, Linda's father proposed champagne for the wedding. Mike's response was, "That stinks. A real man likes to take a drink at a wedding." They ended up with champagne, and Arthur's father, who said he would gladly pay for the liquor, initially refused to attend the wedding. He would be embarrassed with relatives coming from out of town. On the way to the ceremony, he tried to convince one of the ushers to stop at a liquor store.

Arthur fell in love with books early. He went to the library after school a couple of days a week and came home with piles of books. But he wanted to own the ones he liked best. So when Arthur got cash from relatives as presents, he would rush to the bookstore and buy a paperback. This absolutely infuriated his father. Why would his son buy something he could get for free from the library? However, when Arthur desperately wanted to read the bestselling *Rise and Fall of the Third Reich,* which had a long waiting list at the library, Mike found assorted page proofs in the post office's discard bin and tried to assemble a copy.

After Mike died in 1991, Arthur was the executor of his will. In Mike's whole life he had never had a single year in which he earned as much as $20,000. Yet he managed to save almost $90,000 to support his wife after he was gone. He always gave Arthur a few bucks when he went out or headed back to college. He gave him much larger sums when he got married, graduated from college, and took an internship in Washington, DC. But he never bought things for himself. He wore his pants so long they shined. His ties were badly out of date. His collars were frayed. But he bought expensive gifts for his children and grandchildren and loved taking the family out to costly restaurants for special occasions. Every pay day when Arthur was a little boy, his Dad took him to a toy store to buy a present. He relished taking Arthur and Thea and their spouses, and later their children down to the Lower East Side of Manhattan where Jewish store owners sold discounted pocket-books, clothing, yarn, and household appliances.

But when family members brought gifts for him he did not open them. Years later, they could be found still wrapped in his closet. He had a hard time expressing emotions or saying thank you.

Early in their marriage, perhaps for Arthur's parents' 30th anniversary, Linda and Arthur put together all the money they had, including the change they had saved, to buy his parents a Caribbean cruise. This was a long time dream of his mother's. It was a real stretch for them, but Arthur has given few gifts in his life that thrilled him more. On the day the cruise ended, his father called. Arthur excitedly asked, "So how was it?" Mike said, "It was like being in prison. You are stuck on the boat day and night except when you get to a port." Soon after, Arthur and Linda received a package filled with expensive gifts that his dad found at each of the tax-free ports.

Meyer Levine was plain spoken and blunt. The night before Arthur left for college, he gave him a 1-minute sex education briefing in the hallway between his bedroom and the living room. They had never talked about sex before. His dad told him a cat was crossing a railroad track. A train came barreling down. It cut off the cat's tail. The cat went back to find its tail. Along came another train and cut off its head. He said, "Do you see my point?" Arthur looked back blankly. His dad said, "Don't lose your head over a piece of tail." Arthur was entirely inexperienced and had no idea what he was talking about until he said, "So use protection."

Meyer Levine was not inclined to give praise. Arthur once brought home a report card with a grade of 99 in Physics. His father looked at the report card and asked seriously what happened to the other point. He felt people needed to be challenged. They could always do better and he wanted his kids to do better than he had.

When Arthur's first book was published, he sent it to his parents via overnight mail and called his father the next day. Arthur asked what he thought. His dad replied, "It's very short, filled with statistics and will never make *The New York Times* bestseller list." When the book was selected for book of the year in its field, his dad could not say he was proud of Arthur, though it could be seen plainly on his face. Instead, Meyer pulled out the pocket-sized airline schedule he always carried with him after he retired and began planning Arthur's trip to San Diego to accept the award.

Arthur attributes his ambition and driving desire to succeed to trying to impress his father, get him to say he had done well, even though his father has been dead for 2 decades. He realizes too that this was always an impossibility. Had he been elected president of the United States, his dad probably would have said, "So what? Franklin Roosevelt was elected four times."

Mike was a cynical man. He told Arthur every businessman had three sets of books—one for the government, one for his partners, and the real ones—and he believed it. He tended to dislike certain groups of people—women, minorities, foreigners—basically anyone who wasn't Jewish, except Israelis. He didn't like them either; they were foreigners.

This drove Linda crazy. Like Arthur, Linda was a product of the 1960s, and came of age during the Women's Movement. Arthur's father and Linda used somewhat different terminology to describe females. Linda called them *women*, a term that was replacing *girl* in the popular lexicon, while his father used expressions like "hens" and referred to his spouse as the "old battle axe" or "old ball and chain." He would explain to Linda that all hens wanted to do was shop. They were incapable of earning or saving money. They just wanted a male to support them. When Linda and Arthur married, his father told him this was a terrible mistake. She would get pregnant immediately and ruin his career. The fact that she was a 3rd-year law student was irrelevant to his father. That Arthur would even raise this issue was proof of his naiveté about the hen world.

Meyer Levine was a little over 6 feet tall, well-built, attractive, and looked great in a suit. Arthur says he did not inherit many of these characteristics, though he does have his Dad's big ears. Meyer Levine was smart and loved to laugh, but poorly educated and not a reader. With a strong Bronx accent, which Arthur did inherit, he did not have a very good ear for the English language. "Crustaceans" were "crustigens." When Arthur's mom got older and heavier and could not walk even short distances, she insisted on taxicabs. This to Mike was an outrageous request, and he disgustedly called her "the ambulatory invalid."

Mike was also a pedant with an arsenal of lectures on a fairly large range of topics. There were few subjects about which he lacked strong opinions. At the height of the Vietnam War, when college students were desperately trying to avoid the draft and Arthur was involved in antiwar activities, he talked with his Dad about his options. Mike told him that if he got called up and went to Canada or applied for conscientious objector status, he would disown him.

When Arthur received an honorary degree from a college in Taiwan, his father asked how he got there. Arthur said he flew from Boston to Detroit, Detroit to Seoul, and Seoul to Taipei. His father called him "a goddamned idiot," a term he used not infrequently. Mike said his son should have taken a direct flight from Boston to Taiwan. In a smug tone of voice, he said, "You go up once; you go down once." Arthur, in an equally smug tone, countered, there were no direct flights. His father replied, "Then I wouldn't have gone." End of conversation.

The most enduring of Meyer Levine's lectures was the education speech. In contrast to the sex talk, it was a filibuster that could go on for an hour. The moral was, it's essential to attend college. "In life, you are either going to be a jackass or the driver of the jackasses. Anyone can be a jackass like me," he would say. Arthur's friends feared being left alone with his father because they could count on getting the dreaded education lecture, which they had heard many times before. As Arthur got older, the length of the requisite education got progressively longer. After college, his father would scold friends who had only a baccalaureate for dropping out.

Years later, Arthur conducted a study of how poor kids got to college. Among the findings was that each of the students who beat the odds and somehow made it to higher education had a mentor, sometimes a family member, sometimes not, who was a true believer in the efficacy of education, regardless of the amount of education they had themselves. While Arthur was writing the book, he asked his Dad, "How did you know I needed to go to college? None of your friends or the people you work with had gone to college." His answer was a simple "I knew." There was no more to say.

Mike would have liked his son to be an athlete, though he talked about Arthur's accomplishments with anyone he met, just not in front of Arthur. His father loved sports of any kind. He watched them on television or listened to them on the radio year-round. It was his passion. He would have liked his son to be a Heisman Trophy winner who attended West Point. Arthur, unfortunately, was one of the kids who tended to be picked last in most sports at school. He had butterfingers and a propensity to drop the ball, which got worse if his father was watching. Arthur's worst nightmare as a child, which he had repeatedly, was playing a game of catch in which his partner moved progressively further away until Arthur could no longer see him. They kept throwing the ball back and forth. Whatever happened, Arthur knew he could not drop it. He would wake up sweating, pajamas soaked, screaming.

Each year Arthur and his father went to the National Invitational Tournament (NIT) college basketball playoffs at Madison Square Garden. It was a tripleheader; three games that seemed to go on forever—weeks. After the game, they stopped at a local restaurant to have coffee and dessert. Arthur went because he loved making his dad happy, but hated the games. His father went because he thought Arthur loved it, even though they got home very late and his dad ended up with only 4 or 5 hours of sleep before having to get up for work at 5:30 a.m.

Mike retired from the post office as early as he could, but he had nothing to do. He spent hours each day walking the streets. He spent his nights sitting at a card table in the kitchen in a t-shirt, chain smoking, listening to the radio at top volume (his hearing had deteriorated badly), and playing solitaire. He paced back and forth in the kitchen like a tiger in a very small cage. Arthur suggested volunteer work. It would be a chance to meet people and do something to fill his days. Mike looked at Arthur as if he was insane, saying that his time was worth money. If people wanted his help, they would have to pay him.

Arthur and his father became very close in his final years. Today, all kinds of events trigger images for Arthur of his father. Movies are especially powerful. Arthur remembers going with his father to see *The FBI Story, The Man Who Knew Too Much,* and The *Sound of Music,* among many others. For Arthur's birthday, Mike took his son and several friends to see the movie *The Adventures of Davy Crockett,* and bought them all coonskin caps.

Both of his parents had excellent senses of humor. Arthur used the same old jokes with his children, his dad used with him. Mike used to tell him, "I defended you today. Someone told me you weren't fit to live with pigs. I said you were." When he or his sister fell, Mike would distract them from crying by pointing to a crack in the street and saying "Look, you broke the sidewalk. Let's run before the owner catches us." Thea and Arthur would laugh no matter how many times they heard him say it.

But when Arthur thinks of his Dad, it is usually the last several years that come to mind first. His father would walk with him, saying there was something very important they needed to talk about. He just wanted to talk. Arthur would tell him he loved him and kiss him on the forehead. He would ask why Arthur could not catch a later flight and when was he coming back.

* * *

Arthur's mother, Katherine Kalman Levine, called Kittie, was 9 months younger than her husband. Her parents were born in this country; her father's family came to the United States from Romania and her mother's family could be traced back to William Penn. Kittie's mother converted to Judaism at the age of 17 when she married Abie Kalman, who owned a taxi.

Kittie told the story of the children in her grade school class being asked where their parents were born. Her classmates each named a European country. When her turn came, Kittie did too. After class, the teacher asked her why she had done that. Kittie said she did not want her classmates to think her family was too poor to come from Europe.

Arthur's mother had a hard childhood, spending several years in an orphanage when her divorced parents could not care for her and her three younger siblings. A high school graduate with an excellent academic record, Kittie met Mike after the war. They married in 1947, had Arthur 11 months later, and a daughter, Thea, 7 years after that.

Kittie was what was then called a full-time housewife. She earned extra money as a seamstress working at home, making or altering clothes for neighbors, having worked for relatives in the garment industry before marriage. Arthur remembers her feverishly sewing a dress for a customer so she could buy him a cub scout uniform for a meeting that night. Later when Arthur was in high school and Thea in elementary school, his mom took a job as a clerk at the Metropolitan Life Insurance Company in Manhattan.

Kittie was a great cook. She made fantastic potato pancakes, meatballs and spaghetti, and lasagna; Arthur and Thea still try to duplicate her recipes. When they were studying for tests, their mom served fried fish filets or Mrs. Paul's fish sticks—brain food. Thanksgiving was a feast. She made a stuffed turkey, a mashed potato pie with a brown butter crust (to die for), sweet potatoes with marshmallows, candied yams, string bean casserole, and an assortment of pies—apple, cherry, lemon meringue, and pumpkin. Vegetables were her weakness—canned vegetables were boiled until tasteless, and a salad was lettuce covered in salad oil and salt.

The entire family ate dinner together at 5 p.m. each night when Arthur's dad arrived from work. The family did not have a lot of money so by the end of the month, dinners were often hot dogs and eggs.

Kittie Levine was 5 feet 7 inches tall. She was pretty with dark curly hair and lived on coffee and cigarettes, using the coupons that came with her Raleigh cigarettes as well as the green stamps she collected to get the kids skates or appliances for the house. As she got older, Kittie gained a good deal of weight and developed heart problems in her fifties.

She was the family disciplinarian, though she was forever threatening "wait until your father comes home." She was the one who administered punishments and spankings, hitting her children for infractions with whatever was available—shoes, rulers, her hand. She would tell them, "Come here so I can hit you." Arthur came, and Thea ran.

Arthur remembers the worst and most effective punishment his mom ever gave him. She made him stay home from school one day to clean his room because he had not done it despite demands for more than a week, and it looked like a pigsty. To her and to him, this was the nuclear option.

But the strongest tool in his mom's arsenal was guilt. If her children came home late or didn't call, she would tell them she was so worried that she became physically ill and give the details.

More often than not, she covered for the kids, hiding report cards when they were not good enough to show her husband. The unstated quid pro quo was that the children had to cover for her, which meant keeping secrets from their dad generally about purchases that would have infuriated him or occasionally going to a neighborhood store to ask for more credit.

She was a fiercely protective and loving mom. Arthur remembers when he was in college, his mother one day reached out to hold his hand when they crossed the street. She constantly told the world as well as her children, they were the smartest, most attractive, and most accomplished kids in the neighborhood. She believed it too.

Kittie covered the books Arthur wrote with plastic wrap and put them on a shelf for anyone who came to the apartment to see or be shown. But in truth, had he given her a dirty stick instead of a book, she would have wrapped that in plastic and put it on a shelf too. She would have loved it because it came from her children,

Kittie spent more than the family could afford on the kids. Arthur's parents gave him wonderful gifts for his birthday and holidays—a chemistry set, a small pool table, and a microscope—but his mom got him the presents his father would never have permitted, such as an encyclopedia and a much desired 26-volume set of the Warren Commission's testimony, costing $75, which was an extraordinary amount of money at the time and a substantial portion of her husband's weekly salary. Arthur had to keep the Warren Commission reports and the encyclopedia hidden under his bed so his father wouldn't see them.

Kittie opened her home to her children's friends and served as a surrogate parent for them. They asked her advice and would talk to her about things they would never discuss with their own parents. Some friends said they spent more time at her home than they did their own. One ate lunch at Arthur's apartment every school day for a year. Kittie went on class trips, served as the cub scout den leader and arranged for the scouts to decorate bottles with clay and seashells in the Sears department store window.

Nothing was more important than her children's education. When Arthur was young and had a speech defect, his school threatened to transfer him to a school for children with disabilities. Kittie hired a speech therapist to give him lessons at their home instead. When it was discovered that Arthur, who was required to play an instrument for 3 years in middle school, had absolutely no musical ability, his mother paid his music teacher to give Arthur lessons at home. He hated them and never practiced, but the music teacher gave him much better grades than he deserved. When it came time to apply for college and Arthur's entrance test scores were not as high as they needed to be, she sent him to SAT prep courses. His mom worked with him on school projects. For one science fair, she called an uncle who had ties with a major cancer center to arrange for Arthur to participate in a lab study. She later called the same uncle to ask him to pay the college tuition of Arthur and all his cousins, which he did.

The relatives on her father's side were wealthy, having made their money in the garment industry. Arthur's mom never really came to terms with the fact that hers was a working-class family, which was exacerbated by her husband's frugality. She was an impulsive spender, not generally on big ticket items, but mostly on little things—taking taxis instead of public transportation, ordering restaurant meals delivered to her apartment, buying gifts, making long, long distance phone calls to relatives, going out to eat frequently during the day. She concealed bills from her husband. He was embarrassed by walking into neighborhood stores and finding his wife had long overdue accounts. There were calls and letters to collect for unpaid bills.

As an adult, Arthur reacted not by trying to become wealthy, but by trying to avoid dealing with or having to worry about money. Linda paid the bills. When she told him they were spending more money than they were making, Arthur's question was, "How much more do I need to make?" and embarked on a speaking tour. He was never any good at bargaining over prices or negotiating salaries. Borrowing money from family or friends was an anathema. While much of his adult life has been spent fundraising, asking people for millions of dollars, he found it humiliating to ask a friend for $20 to buy a train ticket when he left his wallet at home.

Kittie relished the pleasures of life, large and small. She loved to travel—to see the leaves turning color in New England when Arthur lived in Boston or traveling down the Pacific coast when he moved to California. She would look dreamily at these sites with her eyes shining brightly and pronounce them "bee-u-tiful." Mike took her to Hawaii after he retired. They went to Las Vegas several times. He was enamored of the gambling and she of the shows. Kittie loved being pampered and eating good food, especially lobster, but also cheese and crackers and a glass of wine. She swooned over going to restaurants, whether the high-end establishments Mike liked or the pizza store around the corner.

Katherine Levine died in 1994, a few months after Arthur returned to live in New York. She would have been thrilled that he was home, but was suffering from dementia and no longer recognized him. Thea was an extraordinary daughter, giving Kittie her time, energy, caring, and a place to live through a long illness.

* * *

Although Arthur was a momma's boy, Thea was more independent. He was overjoyed when his parents brought his new sister home from the hospital, having waited so long for a sibling. He greeted her with a pinwheel he made. His parents put it over her crib. They played together as she got older, had the same sense of humor, and shared private jokes and stories. They fought. Arthur drew mustaches on her dolls and told her she was adopted. She hit him with a baseball bat. But above all else, they protected one another. Once when his mom was about to hit him, Thea stepped in front of him and took the slap. After Arthur left for college, he came to New York regularly to smooth the relationship between Thea and her dad. Thea, Arthur, and their dad were all stubborn. Thea was 11 when Arthur left. The geographic distance, age span, and gender difference separated them. They recemented their relationship when Arthur moved back to New York. Thea attended Emerson College and earned a bachelor's degree from City College of New York and a master's degree from Teachers College. Until 2009, she was a teacher in the New York City public schools.

* * *

As a family, the Levines were part of a much larger extended network of relatives—grandparents, uncles, aunts, cousins and even second cousins and their parents. Most lived in the Bronx, though Uncle Whitey, Aunt Helen, and their daughters Sharon and Eva moved to Yonkers, the suburb just over the Bronx border. Arthur thought it was the country. They lived in a house, not an apartment, with a porch, backyard swings, and a garage. It seemed to Arthur an estate rather than the 1950s tract house it really was. Visiting their home was like entering another world. Uncle Max's family moved to California, an unimaginable distance away physically and psychologically. Any time they came to New York was a cause for awe and celebration.

Most Sundays were spent visiting Arthur's paternal grandparents, who also lived in the Bronx. Nine cousins and their parents gathered for an afternoon and dinner. The cousins divided into three groups by age and made a God-awful racket. *Sha* (Yiddish for Shhhh), demanded his grandmother again and again. The family celebrated Passover and the Jewish High Holy days with the grandparents as well, who held an orthodox Passover Seder, ritual and dinner that went long into the night and the kids squirmed and the younger ones cried.

There were also visits with the maternal relatives—more aunts, uncles, and cousins. Two families lived in the Bronx, and the other on Long Island in a commuter suburb of the city. The Long Island visits seemed even more exotic than those to Yonkers.

These frequent visits with relatives should not be viewed through Ozzie-and-Harriet-like lenses, particularly on Mike's side. Grievances, gripes, and jealousies bubbled furiously below and sometimes above the surface. For years, one family did not speak to another.

Traditions were an important part of family life. Arthur's immediate family were nonpracticing orthodox Jews, but proud social Jews. They attended orthodox synagogues on the High Holy days, but were not kosher. Arthur was sent to an orthodox Hebrew school to prepare for his Bar Mitzvah, and his parents spoke Yiddish, but only when they didn't want the children to know what they were saying.

Christian holidays were made secular. There was no Christmas tree, but Mike's birthday was Christmas day, so Santa Claus came every year to bring everyone presents. When Thea put paper Santa Claus's on the living room windows, however, Arthur became furious and ripped them off. She could not do this because they were Jews. Judaism was more than a religion for Arthur's family. In a very real way, it defined who they were.

2

Arthur's Neighborhood

Arthur's apartment building on Creston Avenue and 180th St.

It was a great day. [Johnny and I played in the snow.] When we came back Mark called for me and we played scrabble. . . . Barry called for me, we played scrabble and with my chemistry set. I have to go to bed.

February 5, 1961

I just got home from the dance [first ever dance] It was wonderful. I am in love. . . .We danced cheek to cheek. We went for sodas. She is beautiful. . . . Oh boy, oh boy, wow. . . .

February 24, 1961

I am positive I lost Sheryl (the girl Arthur went to the dance with). . . . What a lousy day.

February 27, 1961, Arthur's seventh grade diary

23

A RTHUR'S NEIGHBORHOOD was a community. It was small in scale, four blocks by eight blocks at its largest, but centered on an area two blocks by four, bordered on the East by the Grand Concourse, intended to be the *Champs d'Elysees* of the Bronx, and on the south by Burnside Avenue with its bakeries, butchers, supermarket, restaurants, 5 & 10 cent store, cleaners, movie theater, and just about anything a family needed. To the west was Jerome Avenue with more stores and a subway to the East Side of Manhattan. The subway to the West Side was on the Grand Concourse. To the north, was Arthur's elementary and junior high school.

As children got older, the boundaries expanded. Going to Hebrew school, the library, or the girl's middle school took children out of the center. High school was a train ride away. Arthur recalls his first subway rides with his friend Barry Bernstein to Manhattan. Barry lived on the third floor of his building and introduced him to stamp collecting and popular music—Bob Dylan, the Beatles, and a host of folksingers. When they fought, Barry would threaten, "I may not get you today. I may not get you tomorrow, but I am going to get you someday when you least expect it." It was a very effective threat. When they first took the subway, they were going to a stamp show and their parents wrote the instructions: "Take the D train to 59th Street. The stop before is 125th Street. Prepare to get off. Walk out the door of the train, which will open on the right. Walk across the platform, about 10 feet. Don't walk up the stairs. Don't stand too close to the yellow warning line. Take the C train, not the. . . ."

Despite its proximity to public transportation, the neighborhood was largely isolated. Few families owned cars. (At age 29, when Arthur got a driver's license, he was the first person in his family to possess one.) Furthermore, ties with the countries most of the families had emigrated from were severed. This was least true for the Irish and near universal for the Jews in the aftermath of the Holocaust.

* * *

Family vacations out of the neighborhood were infrequent. They tended to involve visiting relatives or going to the Catskills, an upstate New York Jewish resort area, segregated by income. The most exciting vacation Arthur ever took was a one-week bus trip with his family to Montreal and Quebec after fourth grade. Although he has since been to countries around the world, none matched this first international trip. He was amazed to find that there was no blue line separating the United States from Canada as appeared on the map at school. People ate different foods. They spoke a different language—French. Stores sold something called Canadian cheese rather than American cheese. He assumed the processed cheese, which he loved, was unique to the United States and sold to countries around the globe.

Arthur's neighbors couldn't afford the kind of vacations middle-class families took. Creston Avenue was populated by working class families and a sprinkling of professionals. Divorce was a mark of shame. Only one girl in his apartment building lived with a single parent. On hot summer nights, because none of the apartments were air-conditioned, the parents sat on the street in chairs brought from their apartments and chatted. The families went to Orchard Beach in the Bronx or the local movie theaters to get relief from the heat.

During the summers, their kids played all day long on the sidewalks and side streets of 180th Street, which was one block long between Creston Avenue and the Concourse. They played stickball, punch ball, and a score of other ball games, which required only an 18-cent, pink rubber Spalding ball, called a *spaldeen,* until it was so dark that they could no longer see. The mark of success was hitting a ball two sewers. Games came to a crashing conclusion when a ball rolled into a sewer. There were kids expert in sewer fishing, using a metal hanger to recover balls.

The kids also played traditional city games—flipping baseball cards; scully (a bottle-cap-based game played on a chalked game board in the street); kick the can (in which a soda can replaced the ball in baseball); hot beans (one child hid a belt and the others had to find it, the child who did, chased the others back to a safety zone, hitting them with the belt as they ran); ringolevio (a team version of hide and seek); Johnny on the pony (in which two teams alternated jumping on each other's backs); and red rover (in which a group of children held arms together and members of an opposing team attempted to break through their line). On rainy days, they played knucks, in which losers had decks of cards slammed on their knuckles. Girls played jump rope and potsy. In fall, the boys played basketball, using the fire escape rungs as the hoop. In winter, the game was football on 180th Street.

Throughout the day, when the ice cream truck arrived at their corner—Bungalow Bar, Good Humor, Mr. Softee—children yelled to parents in the apartment buildings, "Throw down a dime." From the upper floors came socks with change.

When curfews neared, kids yelled up to their parents once again. "Barry's mom said he could stay out later. Can I?" Then Barry would call to his mom, "Arthur's parents said he could stay out later. Can I?" This went on through the evening, until Arthur's parents told him to come in, saying they no longer cared what the other parents allowed their children to do. When he protested, they told him either, "You are our child and you will live by our rules," or "If all the other kids jumped off the Brooklyn Bridge, would you?" He hated when they told him these things, and no doubt his kids hated it when Arthur said that to them.

*   *   *

It was a safe neighborhood, there was little chance of getting hurt, though Arthur received a bloody cut on his forehead requiring stitches when a can took a bad bounce during a game of kick the can. There were cuts and bruises from playing "off the point," a game in which kids threw a ball against the cornice of a building and knuckles occasionally got too close to the building. Arthur still has scars on his hands.

There was also the occasional fight, which involved punching and wrestling, never weapons. Precipitated by "sounding out," trash talk about a kid's mother or arguments about a ballgame, the worst toll was a black eye or a bloody nose. Boys ragged on each other mercilessly, focusing on their greatest vulnerabilities or their mothers. There were slices, sneaking behind a kid and painfully slapping his behind with the back of one's hand, which felt a lot like being struck by a wet towel. There was the double slice, when two kids did it to you simultaneously. But the humiliation was the worst part.

The kids were equally relentless in taunting adults who appeared strange to them. They would chase after an old woman, who dressed in black, yelling "witchy." She in turn called them "kikes," a derogatory term for Jews. Tricks were played on an older man, living in the courtyard, whom they called "Grumpy."

There was the occasional mugging, which increased in frequency after Arthur left for college. Once Arthur's father ran with a bat after a would-be purse thief, who tried to steal a neighbor's handbag. Fortunately for both, Mike didn't catch him.

There were no gangs, though there were periodic rumors that the fabled "Fordham Baldies" were going to raid the neighborhood. The only contact with the police came when the beat cop, who the kids called "Whitey" behind his back, made the kids stop playing stickball, which they believed to be illegal anyway, or told them to break up as they congregated on a corner. The kids and their parents believed the police were there to protect them.

There was no drinking. Drugs were largely unknown, though two local kids died from drug overdoses during and after college. Secretly smoking cigarettes was the biggest vice.

*   *   *

Sex was a mystery to Arthur and most of his friends, though yearning, dirty jokes, macho proclamations, and misinformation were a major feature of his youth. His experience went no further than convincing two girls to kiss him in middle school and having his first serious crush on Debby, a girl who lived in his building. He remembers a date with a cute girl in high school. For months before they actually met, they left notes for each other in the desk of the social studies classroom which they attended at different times. He liked her very much, but when an acquaintance told him she was a "skank," he stopped talking to her and has felt badly about his behavior for decades.

Years later, Arthur found out that a few of the more handsome and sophisticated boys on the block were actually having sex with local girls. By the time this happened, the kids he grew up with were attending different high schools and broke into faster and slower crowds.

*   *   *

Residents lived in the neighborhood for decades and knew each other at least by face. If a child did something wrong or was even rude, his parents knew about it before he got home. One day, Arthur broke three windows accidentally while playing ball with Barry. When he got home, his parents punished him and announced he was starting full-time day camp the next Monday and so was Barry. Even when Arthur grew up, the parental network persisted. Once while living in Boston, he had a half day business trip to New York City and did not have time to visit his parents. While taking the subway to his second appointment, he met a fellow he had known in the old neighborhood, but had not seen in decades. When he got home that night, his mother called telling him how embarrassing it was to hear from the fellow's mother that Arthur had been in New York and had not visited or even told her he was going to be there.

*   *   *

The closest account Arthur ever read of growing up in a world like his was written by a woman from a small town in Iowa. He realized that he had come of age in the equivalent of an urban village. It was not by any means a homogenous village; there were sharp divisions. His friend Jim Welbur described the neighborhood as more of a stew than a melting pot. The population was primarily Jews and Catholics. In Arthur's elementary school class, there were two kids who had religions with names he had never heard of before—an Episcopalian and a Methodist. For him, they were the equivalent of kids from Mars.

The Catholics and Jews played together, but their families didn't socialize. The Catholic kids went to a different school, a parochial school. Occasionally, when angry with the Jewish children they called them "Christ killers." Arthur says one of the consequences of this mix was that while he understood conflicts between Christians and Jews, he couldn't grasp what the Protestant Reformation was about until he met Linda, who is Protestant. He couldn't comprehend what Catholics and Protestants were fighting over or why the Protestants divided into so many different sects. They all believed in Jesus as the messiah, which Jews don't. What was there to be upset about?

Blacks and Latinos in the neighborhood were marginalized. The few Blacks were the cleaning ladies, referred to as "*schwartzes*," meaning Blacks in Yiddish. Puerto Ricans, who more often than not were in service jobs—delivery men, supers, and stock boys—were thought of as undesirable, though the neighborhood children played with the super's daughters, Nelly and Sonia. It was not unusual to hear Puerto Ricans called "spics," the Boricuan equivalent of "kike," behind their backs.

3

Arthur's Education

Future Teacher Club at PS/J.H.S. 79
(Arthur, top row, first from left. Arthur's friend, Jim, top row, third from left)

Today was a rough day. It started off with a high feeling of high marks on my report card . . . but when I got the report card it had an 88 4/10 average [Writing looks to have been altered in diary to elevate grades.]

January 30, 1961

Awful day got a charge [demerit for talking during class] in science and I got a card [home] in Hebrew.

February 28, 1961

Having all my seats changed Better. Larry and I were looking for Sherly [the girl Arthur went to dance with]. We found her, but no more. My marks go down they are worth more than her.

March 8, 1961

I was elected co editor of my science class. I thought Diamond [a teacher
who had given Arthur several charges] would die when I was elected.
March 9, 1961, Arthur's seventh grade diary

DESPITE THE DIFFERENCES among the people living on Creston
Avenue, there was at least one fundamental commonality—
a belief in the power of education and a commitment to the
American dream. It bridged the religious and racial differences. Parents
wanted a better life for their children than they had. That's why they
moved to the neighborhood. Their kids were going to go to college.
This wasn't a hope or expectation. It was a given.

There was a legion of older brothers and sisters in the neighborhood who demonstrated the power of their thinking. Debby's brothers
and sister had gone to college and then law or medical school. Barry's
brother and sister attended the university and became a teacher and a
city inspector.

The few Jewish kids who failed to complete high school or attend
college were known to everyone. It was the equivalent for Arthur's
parents of having been convicted of a crime, and the parents of these
children were universally pitied.

*   *   *

Arthur's parents wanted him to become a doctor. School was the center of their lives. Nothing was more important. Arthur recollects walking down the street with his mom during elementary school. He was
absent from school that day to go to a doctor's appointment. A police-
man passed them, and Arthur was shocked that he didn't arrest him.
That day he realized that a list of all the children who were absent from
school without permission did not go to President Eisenhower every
day as he imagined.

Over dinner each night, his parents asked what happened in school
that day. They talked about his homework and helped him with it
when needed. He was a terrible speller; his parents drilled him end-
lessly on spelling and vocabulary lists. Thea mastered the words more
quickly than Arthur did.

Kittie reviewed his homework. Arthur's handwriting was even
worse than his spelling, which didn't improve until the invention of
"spell check." She made sure his assignments were legible and his
spelling was correct. She went over his math work and told him which
answers were wrong and asked him to try again. She worked with him

on the big projects like science fairs. She calmed him down before tests, which always made Arthur very anxious, causing him to reside in the bathroom for much of the night before. When it was announced that the principal was coming to hear his fourth grade class read the next day, he became nauseous. Kittie was also a class parent who attended school field trips.

* * *

Arthur's mother, and occasionally his dad, went to his school plays, concerts, and open school days to observe his classes. Taking time off from work for his dad was not possible, though he sometimes had weekdays off. His mother attended parent/teacher conferences in the evenings, sometimes with his father, to hear about their son's performance and reported back to him on what they heard. They *kvelled* (a Yiddish word which roughly translates into puff up with pride like a peacock) when the news was good, and when it wasn't, they told him they were disappointed. Teachers complained that Arthur chatted too much during class. On one occasion, his mother was called to school for this reason. This shamed him; he wanted his parents to be proud of him.

More informally, Arthur and his parents ran into his teachers, several of whom lived in the neighborhood when he was in elementary school, on the street or in local stores. This was both astounding and embarrassing to a shy boy, who could not imagine teachers having lives out of the classroom, certainly not intersecting with his own.

* * *

The true test was exam scores and report cards. After every test, his mom asked how he had done. Arthur always thought poorly, but generally did well. They waited for the test results, particularly scores on statewide exams that were required for graduation. The question was never whether Arthur passed, but how high he had scored. His mom was always a cheerleader and sang his praises even when Arthur didn't do well. His father usually thought he could do better, no matter what the score.

Kittie seemed to know exactly the day report cards would be issued, and she studied it closely when Arthur brought one home. She went over the report card with him class by class, grade by grade. His dad, when Kittie shared the report card with him, perused it and put it down on the table when he finished, with either an admonition or no comment. Good grades were shared with relatives and neighbors, and parents in return shared them with their children. "Did you know that your cousin Edward got a ninety-eight on chemistry Regents [the New York state-wide exam]?"

*   *   *

Arthur attended P.S. 79 and all boys J.H.S. 79. The classes in his elementary school were organized according to the children's ability. There were three classes in each grade, the "1" class was the highest ability and the "3" class was the lowest. What mattered most on graduation day at the end of each academic year was that Arthur be placed in the "1" class, which he was.

In entering junior high school, the mark of excellence was being placed in the special progress class, in which students advanced through middle school in 2 years rather than 3. Arthur was not chosen for the program. His mom soothed him and his father said nothing.

For high school, success meant being admitted to a selective high school. Arthur was chosen for the Bronx High School of Science. His mother bought him a huge steak to celebrate, and his father may have congratulated him.

The next hurdle was higher education. There were standards and expectations here too. Few children in the neighborhood went to private colleges. A minority attended out of town public universities. Their families could not afford such schools. City College of New York, which was free, demanded the highest grades and test scores of the commuter public universities, so it was the place to go. Other local public universities were greeted as good, but not marks of highest distinction for the students who attended them. Attending a community college, while better than not going to college, was seen as evidence that a student had not performed well in high school.

4

Leaving the Bronx

ARTHUR LEVINE   FO 7-7190
2078 Creston Ave., Bx. 53
Forum, Hall Sq., Lunchroom
Sq., Spanish Club

Arthur, High School Yearbook Picture

55% of the students at Cornell are from Iowa.
College Admissions Guide, 1965

ARTHUR LEFT THE BRONX to go to college, and he didn't return to the Bronx because he had gone to college.

Arthur had certain advantages in getting to college. He had good grades and test scores. He attended a high school where all 900 students who graduated with him went to college. And his mother's uncle paid the full cost of his tuition, room and board. These factors had much more to do with *where* Arthur went to college than *whether* he went to college.

But he had the same disadvantages facing most would-be first generation college students. He and his family knew nothing about college except that Arthur was going there after high school. They had no idea how one got from high school to college.

In a high school junior-year guidance session for students and their parents, they learned that you had to apply to college. It was not like being promoted to the next grade. They had to write to the colleges for catalogs and applications. What kind of letter should they write? they wondered.

It had long been assumed that Arthur would attend City College, but that changed when Uncle Henry said he would pay for his education. All colleges were possible now, but Arthur's family didn't know how you chose which colleges to apply to. The only contact they had had with higher education was when Arthur and his friends were thrown off the New York University campus in the Bronx, across the street from the public library. "Townies," as they were called, were not welcome there.

The only knowledge his family had of institutions of higher education came from watching television—college sports and a quiz show named *College Bowl,* which invariably included short profiles of the colleges playing. Arthur had fallen in love with Villanova, which had always been a dark horse at the NIT playoffs and did remarkably well. He was crushed to learn it was a Catholic school.

His parents talked to relatives and neighbors who had already sent children to college. They asked what were the best colleges in America. They got a lot of answers, but Harvard, and Brandeis—a Jewish college—were the most common. Arthur suspects that if they had spoken to families across the street, Notre Dame would have won.

They bought a college guide and pored over the catalogs. Cornell was especially appealing because Arthur had won a Regents scholarship, which could only be used in-state. Arthur and his mom were dumbfounded to learn that 55% of its students came from Iowa. Days later, when they accidentally turned to the wrong page in the guide, they realized there were two Cornells, one in New York and the other near Cedar Rapids, Iowa.

Arthur heard the other kids at school talk about colleges. His friend Harvey told him Syracuse University was the place to go.

He visited the high school college guidance counselor. Bronx Science only allowed its students to apply to three colleges and the City University of New York. He brought his list of three schools to the meeting, which included Pennsylvania State University, which at the time he thought was the University of Pennsylvania. She told him he couldn't get into any of the schools and recommended he apply to Beloit, a liberal arts college in Wisconsin. For a boy who had only been to Pennsylvania, New Jersey, and New York, this was like being told he needed to go to college on the moon. He left her office teary-eyed.

In the end, he ignored her advice, and the family chose a serendipitous, truly random set of schools, which most certainly would have changed had he applied a week earlier or later. Preparing essays and applications to Cornell, Brandeis, and Syracuse was a family project. Recommendations were required. Arthur asked his math teacher, who reviewed the application and declined, saying there was nothing in the application that would encourage any school to want him. Again, he left an office crushed.

Arthur's father wanted him to apply to Harvard. Arthur was afraid to, a kid like him had no right to apply to Harvard. Plus, he thought he would not be admitted, which he learned later was entirely correct. Mike told him, "You can't get rejected if you don't apply." He said this to Arthur again and again throughout his adult life when encouraging him to undertake challenges he feared, often rightfully. When Arthur did not apply, his dad called him a coward and "a goddamned idiot."

They only visited one school, Brandeis, where an interview was either required or suggested. Arthur and his dad took the train to Boston's North Station and a second train from South Station to the Waltham campus. On the way, they passed through states, where Arthur had never before been—Connecticut, Rhode Island, and Massachusetts. Brandeis seemed so far away. From the tracks of the Brandeis train stop, they trudged through a snow storm to the admissions office. The storm made a campus tour impossible. Arthur had an interview, but felt he and his family were entirely out of place at Brandeis.

Applications were filed in January and the whole family waited for answers on April 15. They were told by friends and neighbors that a thin letter meant rejection and fat envelopes were acceptances. Arthur's mother waited for the mailman every day as the 15th approached. He came home on the day admissions letters were due and his mother said there is good news and bad news. He had been rejected by Cornell and accepted by Brandeis and City College. Arthur is still waiting to hear from Syracuse. They didn't know which of the schools he should attend. After consulting with everyone they knew, they selected Brandeis.

The family spent the summer before college reading and rereading and rereading again every correspondence from Brandeis, looking for secret messages on the order of the *The DaVinci Code*. They went to the Lower East Side to buy a trunk and a new wardrobe for Arthur and shipped them to Brandeis as the fall approached.

* * *

On the designated day, the entire family boarded the train to Boston. All Arthur remembers of the trip is that he had two or three huge pimples on his face. They arrived on campus and went to his dormitory room. It was a triple. Arthur was the last one to arrive and got the upper bunk.

After unpacking his trunk and suitcases, his family departed for home. They hugged and kissed him, said goodbye, and then just left him there. He had never before been away from home, other than an overnight at Aunt Helen's. He felt abandoned.

His two roommates—John from Massachusetts and Steve from Pennsylvania—both had a number of friends on campus or nearby. Arthur had none. The roommates were very different than him. John was Catholic and a drinker, and had attended a private school. Steve had taken a gazillion Advanced Placement classes; was looking for "gut" courses, whatever that meant; and began meeting with professors immediately after arriving at Brandeis.

The upperclassmen next door had women in their room and were playing a song on their stereo with the repeated line, "Baby, let me bang your box."

Later in the day, there was a talk by his residence counselor, a Brandeis senior. He spoke about the rules regarding parietals, sex, drinking, and drugs, which alternately confounded and shocked Arthur. He closed the session by saying, "Don't do anything I don't do. If you don't know what I do, then be as discrete as I am."

That night, there was a gala, welcoming the new students to Brandeis. It was pouring when the event ended and Arthur, sopping wet, got lost trying to find his dormitory. He cried. He went home four times before Thanksgiving.

* * *

The saving grace for Arthur in attending Brandeis was that the overwhelming number of students were Jewish. For him, this commonality clouded the socioeconomic gap between him and the friends he made. Jack from New Hampshire's dad was a doctor. Mike, who said he was born with a platinum spoon in his mouth, also had a doctor for a father. Norm's mom was a physics professor, and his father was a teacher. John's mother was an investor.

Arthur vividly remembers visiting John's home on New York's Park Avenue during his senior year of college. John's building had things Arthur had never seen before—a doorman and an elevator that opened directly into his apartment, which had a spare room, called the maid's room, original art works, and even a sculpted bust of John. Arthur was overwhelmed. He never imagined people lived like that. In the years since, he's been in the homes of some of America's wealthiest families, but none impressed him as much as John's.

As an adult, Arthur has regularly found gaps in his knowledge that children who grew up in middle- and upper-class families learned. Until he met Linda, Arthur had no idea how people bought cars or houses, that they didn't pay the full price on the day of purchase but took loans. He didn't know what a mortgage was. A couple of years ago, when his shirt collar kept popping up, someone told him he had forgotten his collar stays. He had no idea what they were.

*   *   *

Four years after enrolling at college, Arthur graduated. He loved Brandeis and the frequent visits home ceased after the first term. Although he majored in biology, Arthur did not go on to medical school, which was a major disappointment to his parents, though not to the medical schools. Instead, Arthur fell in love with colleges and universities and wanted a career studying them and someday heading one. He spent the 2 years immediately after college working at a series of odd jobs as a night watchman, a telephone salesman, and substitute teacher, while carrying out a study with John of undergraduate education around the country. This led to his first book and a job doing research on higher education at the Carnegie Council on Policy Studies in Higher Education and its successor, the Carnegie Foundation for the Advancement of Teaching. Along the way, Arthur earned a doctorate in sociology and higher education from the State University of New York, Buffalo. After Carnegie, he became president of Bradford College in Massachusetts and then a faculty member at the Harvard Graduate School of Education. His next job was president of Teachers College, Columbia University. He is now president of the Woodrow Wilson National Fellowship Foundation in Princeton, New Jersey.

*   *   *

Arthur married Linda Fentiman in 1974, and they have two daughters—Jamie, who was born in 1979, and Rachel, who was born in 1986, the same year Leonel Disla was born.

Arthur describes himself as a 1960s leftover who chose education as a career because he believed that education is the only effective way to improve the world. It is the principal vehicle for giving low-income kids a chance at a better life.

5

A Homecoming

Arthur, President of Teachers College

I returned . . . with a profound sense of loss. What I visited was not the old neighborhood I remembered and cherished. Of all the places I had ever lived, I still thought of the old neighborhood as home. It was no longer a physical location, just a memory. . . . The fundamental difference between my old neighborhood and its current incarnation is that the American dream died.

Arthur on his first visit to the Bronx in fall 1994

I N 1970, ARTHUR GRADUATED from college and his parents moved to Queens, which, he says, is closer than China, but does not appear so to Bronx residents. Aside from visits to his parents and business trips, Arthur did not return to New York City for 28 years—until 1994, when he became president of Teachers College.

One of his first stops was the "old neighborhood." Arthur had lived in many places—California, Connecticut, Maine, Massachusetts, Virginia, western New York, and Washington, DC—but no place felt more like home to him than the "old neighborhood." On his first visit, he walked around the old school yard where he had played ball. It was littered with broken glass, the occasional used condom, and empty crack vials. There were enough vials to fill a baggie. On this and future visits, Arthur brought a couple of vials back to his office as a reminder of the challenges facing Teachers College. They were always gone the next day. Arthur joked that the physical plant staff was trying to protect his reputation.

He walked the block from his school to his old apartment building. All he could see and hear were the changes. The smells and sounds of the neighborhood were different. Spanish was the language of the street, not English or Yiddish. There were more graffiti, more trash on the street, and overflowing garbage pails on the corners. There were now a massive iron gate on the front of his old apartment building and piles of rubble where the apartment building across the street had stood. Arthur's friends Audrey, Terry, and Neila had lived there. As he walked around, Arthur found familiar haunts were gone—the pool hall, which allowed him and his friends to play when they were underage; the movie theater where they were thrown out for running up and down the aisles screaming; the ice cream parlor where he took his first dates; and the bagel factory where he and his father bought hot bagels on Sunday mornings along with the *Daily News.*

There were a lot of men on the street. They stared at Arthur in his suit and tie or at least he thought they did. Arthur had walked down this street thousands of times in the past. He had never before been afraid.

* * *

Arthur experienced a profound sense of loss. What he had visited was not the old neighborhood of his memory. He was angry, not with anyone in particular, but with the world. After a peripatetic life, the one place he thought of as home, the physical constant in his life, had vanished.

It was, of course, foolish for him to expect that it would not have changed profoundly after 40 years, but he really wanted it to be the same. It reminded Arthur of alumnae returning for their 25th reunions at Bradford College, where he had been president. They had become middle aged. They saw the changes in their appearance in the mirror. Their kids had left for college. Their husbands were not Prince Charming and their dreams had given way to realities. They needed for their alma mater to be as they remembered it, a touchstone with their youth and a world of endless possibilities. When it wasn't, they were angry and had endless complaints. This always seemed the unhappiest class at reunions to Arthur.

Arthur's subsequent visits were less emotional and, he liked to believe, had more to do with reality. As he learned more about his old neighborhood, he found that nostalgia had a magical ability to smooth edges, make some memories shine and induce amnesia regarding others.

On the second visit, the things that hadn't changed became clearer. Arthur saw that most of the buildings he grew up with were still there—his apartment building, his school, the stores, synagogues, and churches. So were the streets where he used to play ball, the library, and the subway stations. Often they were used for different purposes though. The synagogue, where Arthur had his Bar Mitzvah, was now a church, and the Jewish deli, which had the best pastrami he'd ever eaten, had become a bodega. There was no mistaking it. Physically, it was still the old neighborhood; more neglected and rundown, but still the old neighborhood.

*   *   *

The neighborhood had faced hard times in the years since Arthur left for college. Working class Whites began moving away even before he did and were replaced by minorities. The departures turned into an exodus with the opening of Co-op City—the largest closed community in the country with 15,372 affordable units in the north Bronx. Local businesses followed. In 1959, there were 2,000 manufacturers in the South Bronx. Fifteen years later, there were 650. Nearly 18,000 jobs were lost. This was compounded by a recession in the mid-1970s and the export of America's manufacturing industries, a staple of immigrant employment, to other countries.

In the South Bronx, arson boomed as a means for landlords to collect insurance on properties plunging in value and for residents to receive relocation fees, allowing them to leave deteriorating and dangerous tenements. Between 1970 and 1980, 30,000 buildings were abandoned and burnt in the Bronx. There was an average of 33 fires a night between 1970 and 1975. Violent crime spiked. The city adopted a policy of "Planned Shrinkage"—cutting services such as sanitation, health, education, transportation, police, and fire prevention—to encourage residents to leave.

Banks stopped investing in the South Bronx; new mortgages dropped by 85%. Existing mortgages were sold for as little as a 1/10 of a cent on the dollar. Branch banks closed on the major thoroughfares.

A blackout in July 1977 came to symbolize the decline. Pictures of broken windows, trashed stores, and massive looting were broadcast across the nation. To save his store, a Burnside Avenue butcher stood outside its door on the roof of his car with a shotgun in hand, ready to shoot anyone who tried to loot his business. When the blackout ended, in the course of 25 hours there had been 307 fires and 473 looted businesses in the Bronx. Burnside Avenue looked like a war zone.

A crack epidemic followed in the 1980s. Then out of the ashes, with an improving economy and public and private investment, the old neighborhood began to stabilize.

This was the world Arthur returned to. The residents in his old neighborhood had changed. They were now poor and largely Hispanic and Black. Caucasians made up less than 2% of the population. Seven out of ten residents were Hispanic. More than one out of every five were Black. A greater proportion (45%) of the population was born abroad, largely in the Caribbean and Latin America.

Median family income declined, according to the 2000 census, since he left the neighborhood, to $24,633 ($30,798 in current dollars), which is half the national average.[1] The buying power of minimum wage jobs, which many in the neighborhood held, dropped substantially.[2] A third of all families were living below the poverty line and the unemployment rate had nearly tripled.

While educational attainment of neighborhood adults had risen since 1960, it has actually dropped significantly relative to the rest of the nation. When Arthur was in seventh grade in 1960, 40% of the adults in the neighborhood had graduated from high school, which was one percentage point below the national average. Now half the adults in the neighborhood reported having completed high school in comparison with the 87% graduation rate nationally.[3]

Families changed too. The divorce/separation rate increased sevenfold in the neighborhood. In 1960, 6% of all children were living in a family without both parents. In 2000, 46% of all families were headed by a female without a husband. Children today live in a world in which they are more independent and have less adult supervision than was true decades ago.

The neighborhood was also a more dangerous place. Gangs, violent crime, beatings, shootings, and stabbings were everyday realities. Children describe their world this way, and the police blotters confirm their accounts: "I have seen guns. I have seen people crying because they have been stabbed. I have seen death, bodies on the floor killed by a gun shot." Children went to more funerals than weddings.

* * *

But the fundamental difference between Arthur's neighborhood then and now is that the American dream has died. When Arthur lived there, the American dream was the neighborhood religion. Jews and Catholics and the handful of Protestants who lived there worshipped it. Parents and children alike knew that with education and hard work, children could have something better than their parents. Though most of the neighborhood parents had never finished high school, Arthur and his friends knew they were going to college with the certainty that they would be having breakfast the next day. There was a long line of youngsters—brothers, sisters, neighbors, relatives, and friends—ahead of them who had made the trek from the neighborhood to the middle class and showed that it could be done. There was also the sprinkling of professionals living in the neighborhood—a doctor, a dentist, and many teachers. And most of Arthur's friends followed in their footsteps, aware of those who had fallen along the way, their missteps to be avoided. In the end, Marvin and Eddie became doctors. Jimmy became a school principal, and Barry, a teacher. Jay became a lawyer, and Debby, a nurse. Steven became a Wall Street investor. Elliot went to work for the federal government. Terry went to Harvard and was never heard from again.

But today the dream has disappeared. The highway to mobility is gone. Any child who moves up and out must create the road for her- or himself much as the first pioneers did going west. Most of the children are consigned to remain in a world of poverty, with inadequate educations, dead-end jobs, and violence. This is the world where Leonel Disla grew up and died.

PART II

LEO'S STORY

6

Leo's Parents

Leo, dancing with his mom shortly after moving to New York

My mom alway is working hard. Her goal for us was to get a better life. To have ours life easier than hers. When she dont have a job she feel uncostuble. She had never been in a job that pay at hour $7.00 never. Getting low pay checks she gave us everything we need it when we were small.

Spring 2002

My dad . . . I use to thing [think] that he was a bad father because I didn't knew him that much but know he's a good father now that I get to hang out with him he don't get mad at anything I do he respet me. . . . I have fun with him

Leo's Diary, Summer, 2004

L EONEL DISLA (LEO) was born in the Dominican Republic in 1986 and immigrated to the United States when he was 8. Three years later, he and his mother, older brother, and younger sister moved to Creston Avenue.

Leo's parents met in the Dominican Republic when his mom, Miriam, was a teenager. His dad, Andre, a few years older, had been with many women before her, but Miriam was the first he was ever serious about. She was quiet and studious, while Andre, or Moreno as everyone called him because of his dark skin, was charismatic, confident, and charming. He took her to his favorite beaches and discotecas and treated her to drinks and desserts. She fell in love with him.

Miriam dreamed of having a family with Moreno and living in a house made of cement *bloques* instead of the dilapidated wooden home where she grew up. She didn't want her kids picking yams in *el campo* and selling them at the market like her brothers. Instead she imagined her children going to college and having a *profesión*. But Miriam's most immediate dream was to get out of her house. Her father was an alcoholic, and although he had become less violent in recent years, the scars on her body were lifelong reminders of the terrifying nights he'd come home drunk and abuse her.

Miriam and Moreno were boyfriend and girlfriend for more than a year and a half before they moved in together. It wasn't the brick home she dreamt of, but a small wooden one with a cement floor. Miriam didn't care; she was thrilled.

Miriam was the first in her family to graduate from high school. Her older brothers quit years earlier to support the family. The only reason Miriam was able to stay in school was because her mom found a job as a high school janitor. She used her monthly salary of 30 Dominican pesos (about $1 U.S) a month to pay for Miriam's school fees. Miriam loved school so much that she was one of the first in her neighborhood to register for a postsecondary education program in teaching. Her neighbors marveled at how hard she studied.

Moreno wasn't as big a fan of formal schooling. He had quit school as a little boy and made money working with cars. Cars were his passion, and he had worked on them ever since his first job. He supported his mom and Miriam by fixing and selling tires.

When Miriam found out that she was pregnant, both she and Moreno were ecstatic. He hoped for a son, and she hoped that Moreno would be around more. He usually alternated between sleeping at their house and at his mom's house. Some mornings Miriam felt so nauseous she thought she was going to pass out. But she continued going to school and managed to earn her degree in teaching. Three months later, Miriam gave birth to her first child. He weighed close to 10 pounds, and they named him Lisandro. He was the spitting image of his father.

After Lisandro's birth, Moreno spent most nights at his mom's house where he could freely bring women. He'd stumble back to Miriam the next day, smelling of liquor. She'd yell at him. He'd ignore her. Since he was the man of the house—the one making the money—he felt justified in going out whenever and with whomever he wanted. Moreno became careless about hiding his affairs, and Miriam got so mad at him once that she cut up all of his clothes. They fought almost every day, right up until Moreno left for Puerto Rico. He heard there was money to be made in the neighboring island.

* * *

To get help caring for Lisandro, Miriam moved home with her mother, Teresa, who had been taking care of kids ever since she had her first child at 13. Life became a blur of feeding the extended family, changing diapers, and cleaning. When Miriam had time, desperately wanting to support her family, she searched for a teaching position. But with the country's almost 30% unemployment rate, Miriam couldn't find a job, even with her teaching degree.

Moreno returned to the Dominican Republic and, 8 months later, Miriam was pregnant again. Moreno wanted as many children as possible. Miriam was hopeful that a second child would improve their relationship. But Moreno was more interested in adventures than fulfilling Miriam's wishes. For years friends and neighbors who had been to New York had told Moreno, "*Si se muere sin conocer Nueva York, se muere un ciego*" ("If you die without knowing New York, you die a blind man"). They made it sound like in New York money grew on trees. For Dominicans, getting a U.S. tourist visa was like playing the lottery since few who applied received them. But Moreno had the right connections in Puerto Rico. His second son was born on June 8, 1986. Leonel (Leo) was a happy beautiful baby with huge brown eyes and dark thick lashes.

Soon after Leo was born, Moreno bought a plane ticket for New York, packed a suitcase, and left with promises of keeping in touch. He stayed at a friend's apartment in the upper Manhattan neighborhood of Washington Heights. The sounds of *Bachata*, the music blasting from car stereos, the many Dominican restaurants, and the large Dominican population living in the area made Moreno feel at home. His friend introduced him to new friends, and through his connections he got an apartment and a job "off the books" fixing elevators and cars. Moreno sent some money home to his family, but used most of it to buy a car, go out with friends, and romance women.

After about 9 months, Moreno called Miriam to tell her he was coming home. She couldn't wait to see him. Even though they fought and she didn't like his fooling around, Miriam was lonely. She missed him. Once again, he spent some nights with Miriam and a lot more at his mom's house. Miriam announced she was pregnant. Two months later, one of the women Moreno slept with also got pregnant. Moreno tried to keep the women from finding out about each other, but too many neighbors gossiped. Miriam cried and screamed at him. He decided to go back to New York City. He could make more money there in a week than an entire month in his country. During his first attempt to return to the United States, Moreno went through Puerto Rico, but got caught and sent home. On his second attempt, he bought a ticket to Costa Rica, but returned 5 months later when he realized how far it was from the United States. Shortly after, Miriam gave birth to his first daughter, Iliana (Maholi). Then, his girlfriend gave birth to his second daughter. Moreno wanted to return to the United States more than ever.

Moreno finally saved enough money to fly to Mexico City, where he drove from the capital to the border of the United States. He paid a "coyote" $5,000 Dominican dollars (roughly $175 American) to bring him over the border. They drove from Tijuana to San Diego, where Moreno flew to New York, with a short stopover in Chicago. Twenty thousand Dominican dollars ($666 American) and 3 sleepless nights later, Moreno had made it back to New York City. This time he lived in a basement apartment and made his money dealing motorcycles. He stayed in the United States from 1988 to 1995.

*   *   *

Back in the Dominican Republic, Miriam and her three kids survived on the roughly $10 to $15 a day her brothers made doing factory and construction work. Miriam wanted a better life for her kids but felt stuck. She had been looking for a teaching job for 3 years and had only gotten one offer. When she found out where the school was located, her heart sank. It was too far from her house. Even if she had taken it, the most she might have made was around $80 (U.S. dollars) a month. One of her brothers, on the other hand, had been in the United States since the 1980s. He sent enough money each month so that their family was able to reconstruct their wooden shack to a home with brick walls and a cement floor. Miriam looked at her neighbors' houses. Many were old dilapidated wooden structures. Others that were freshly painted houses made of cement *bloques* were owned for the most part by neighbors who had lived in the United States, or had relatives there. Miriam decided that she wanted to move to New York.

It took a year to plan her trip. When it was time to go, she hugged and kissed her kids goodbye and told them that she was going to "La Capital" (Santo Domingo) instead of the United States. She didn't want them to be scared that she was so far away. Miriam says, walking away was the hardest thing she had ever done. She had no idea when or if she would ever see her children again. But the possibility of a better life for her family gave her the courage to leave. Miriam prayed and cried throughout her journey to the United States.

* * *

Moreno met Miriam at John F. Kennedy Airport. She stepped cautiously onto the escalator, not sure how it worked since she had never been on one before. On their way to Washington Heights, she looked out the taxicab window, amazed to see street lights on every corner. When they got out of the taxi, Miriam stepped into snow for the first time. When she entered Moreno's one-room apartment, it felt strange to be so closed in.

Moreno introduced Miriam to his friends in the neighborhood, who helped her get acquainted with *Alto Manhattan* (Upper Manhattan). They showed her how to use the subway and told her which local stores sold yucca, platanos, and the cheapest rice and beans. A neighbor helped her get her first full-time job. For a little over $5.00 an hour, Miriam worked 8 hours a day in a rundown warehouse sewing pearls onto clothes. When the factory shut down, her workmates told her about a sunglass factory, where she got her second job. Miriam worked the nightshift, putting stickers on sunglasses. Moreno couldn't understand why Miriam worked at night. "Only prostitutes work at night," he scoffed. While she was bringing home around $200 a week, Moreno was making around $700 a week acquiring and selling motorcycles. She was happy. For the first time in her life, she was making her own money. Her dream was to save enough to build a cement house in the Dominican Republic. Her immediate priority was bringing her children to the United States.

Through Miriam's social network, she got help with the necessary documentation for her kids to live in the United States. She filled out visa applications for her kids, saved enough money as proof of income to support them, and went through the Immigration and Naturalization Service hoops to bring her kids to the United States. Moreno never wanted their kids to move. He didn't think New York was a good place to raise children. But Miriam missed them too much to listen or agree.

Some Dominican parents waited years before all of the paperwork went through, forcing them to miss some of the most crucial years of their children's development. Miriam was unusually lucky; it only took a year. She returned to the Dominican Republic, packed up her kids and brought them back with her to New York. Lisandro was 10 years old, Leo was 8, and Maholi was 6. During their first year, the family stayed in Moreno's basement apartment. Leo didn't remember much, except that his entire family slept in one room. He also remembered feeling very lonely and bored. In the Dominican Republic, Leo could play outside anytime he wanted. But in New York he could only go outside with his mom, who was usually working. School was also a big adjustment. Leo and Lisandro were held back a year so that they could learn English. Leo hated speaking English; it was embarrassing to speak so poorly and he was afraid people would laugh at him.

*   *   *

Usually it was Miriam and Maholi who did the grocery shopping at the local supermarkets catering to Dominicans. During one of their outings, Maholi saw a little girl, who looked exactly like her. The little girl asked her mom, "Mami, how come I look so much like that girl?" Miriam's heart dropped. She hadn't seen Moreno's former girlfriend since she left the Dominican Republic. Miriam told Maholi, "This is your half sister. Give her a hug." Maholi gave the girl an awkward hug before they walked away.

Moreno and Miriam's relationship was worse in the United States than in the Dominican Republic. The only difference was that Miriam was making her own money. So when Moreno moved back to the Dominican Republic, Miriam stayed in New York with the kids and ended their relationship. Since she only made $960 a month, Miriam had to move to an affordable one-bedroom apartment in the Bronx. But after finding homeless people passed out in the entryway of the building, the family moved to another one-bedroom apartment on 182nd Street and Creston Avenue. Miriam couldn't afford the $600 rent, so she rented the bedroom to a border. She made the entryway the living room and divided the living room into two bedrooms. Leo, Lisandro, and Maholi slept in one section of the room and Miriam slept in the other.

Of the many borders who rented the room for $125 a week, Tony was Leo's favorite. He was a young attractive Latino who always wore the latest name-brand clothes and came home with a different girl every night. Tony was equally fond of Leo. When Leo's coat was stolen, Tony took out his gun and offered to find the thieves. Although Leo declined, he was moved by the offer. Tony rented the room for about a year before moving out. The family kept in touch with him even after Tony was jailed for selling crack/cocaine. Following Tony, the stream of tenants moving in and out blended together for Leo. None of them were as cool as Tony.

*   *   *

Money was a constant worry for Miriam, and she paid her bills in order of urgency, using every penny for rent, food, electricity, phone, cable, and the kids' expenses. Moreno never sent money since it wasn't worth much in the United States. Leo sympathetically observed, "The whole time we lived in New York, I never seen my mom spend money on herself unless she needed something like a coat. And I ain't ever see her go out on the weekend. Not once."

Even if Miriam wanted to go out, she didn't have the time. Miriam left her apartment for work at 1:30 p.m. After traveling 2 hours to New Jersey, she punched in at 4 p.m. and made small boxes for chocolates on an assembly line for 10 hours each day. She clocked out at 2 a.m. and arrived home around 4 a.m. On the days Miriam wasn't working, she cleaned the apartment, washed clothes, and cooked enough food for the week so that her kids had something to eat when they got home from school. Her arms were often swollen from the repetitive motion her work demanded. She suffered from back and leg pain from standing all day. Leo gave her foot massages to help ease the pain.

Near Christmas, Miriam got laid off. She took a train and two buses to the unemployment office in New Jersey where she received $123 per week in benefits, about half of her usual salary. Miriam called friends and relatives to see if they knew of any jobs, and she spent 1 day each week going from factory to factory filling out applications. She would have gone every day, but couldn't afford the transportation. Several months later, the chocolate factory began hiring again, and Miriam resumed her previous job. The only difference was they increased the expected production per hour. She wanted to look for another job, but there wasn't time. If she took days off from her factory job, her family didn't eat.

*   *   *

Miriam wanted a different job that would allow her to see her kids during the week. She thought if she spoke English, she could get a better job. So Miriam signed up for a free English class at her local community center from 9 a.m. to 12 p.m. Between school and work, Miriam was getting 4 hours of sleep a night. Exhaustion forced her to quit the class after 2 weeks.

The only time Miriam saw her kids was on the weekends. When Leo's principal called to talk about a problem at school, she was rarely home. Even when the school sent notices in the mail, Leo got to the mailbox before his mom. Miriam felt like she was losing control of her kids by the time Leo was in sixth grade, Lisandro was in eighth grade, and Maholi in fourth grade. Lisandro began going to parties, and Miriam insisted that he be home at midnight. When he complained that none of his friends had curfews, she stood firm, and the two argued until Lisandro stormed out of the apartment. The first time he broke his curfew, Miriam forbid him to go out. But Miriam finally gave up when he continued coming home past midnight. When Leo started going to parties with his brother, Miriam tried to reinstate the curfew, but they didn't listen. By the age of 13, Leo often stayed out until 3 or 4 in the morning.

*   *   *

Regardless of the hardships Miriam faced as a single mom, she believed in the Dominican dream. With hard work and discipline, she was determined to build a new house in the Dominican Republic for her family. It would be custom made, and the children would each have their own bedrooms. She imagined a kitchen with new appliances and a front porch where she and her family could sit and talk with the neighbors.

Her children had already accomplished one of her dreams. They spoke English, an unlikely achievement had they stayed in the Dominican Republic. Miriam wanted her kids to graduate from an American school where they could study for whatever profession they wanted. Then they could get a job they liked, not just whatever job they could get. And then her grandchildren would have an even better life than theirs. That's what pushed her to work so hard.

7

Leo's Neighborhood and His Education

Leo and his mom on the PS 79 playground, fifth-grade graduation

My goal in geting out of H.S. is one of the most important to my family. They want to see me graduating from H.S. and college. . . After I get out of Junior hight school I'm trying to foget the pass and start something knew. To fogget about how many times I got lelf back and how teacher or I use to treat them.

Spring 2002

Almost all the girls from my class are not Virgin and they are from 13 to 15 year old. Of the people that I hang out with, boys and girls, they are like an 85% ore 90% Percent that alredy are having sex. So around here a 12 year old boy or girl having sex is not a big deal. I mean for us is not a big deal but for they parent is a big deal. My mom she allways tells me to use condom when I going to have sex. To my littler sister my mom just said to her to don't have sex with anyone. My mom don't even let her have a boyfriend. So girls are different.

Leo's Diary, Fall, 2001

L EO'S EDUCATION OCCURRED as much on the streets as it did in school. One day, he and his friend Pedro headed to the basketball hoop on the corner of Burnside and Creston Avenue. Leo was 12 years old and wore an extra large baggy t-shirt and a basketball jersey. His jeans were so baggy that he pinned the bottoms to his sneakers with thumbtacks and was constantly pulling the sagging jeans up around his hips. Basketball was Leo's favorite sport, and that corner was the best place to play because everyone from the block hung out there.

They passed several drug dealers on the way, avoiding the piles of garbage and dog droppings that littered the sidewalk. Merengue and bachata music blared from the open windows of several apartments and parked cars. They said hello to the older men sitting on milk boxes on the street playing a game of dominos on a makeshift table.

Leo noticed a kid across the street staring at him. He tried to remember how they knew each other. A party? A basketball game? When the teenager crossed the street, Leo figured he was going to say hello. Instead the kid socked him. Before he could react, a group of "Crime Fam" gang members jumped him. One guy punched him in the eye four times, another kicked him in the ribs, and a third hit Leo in the arm.

Pedro stood immobile, watching his friend take a beating that was meant for him. The day before, Pedro had gotten into a fight with a kid name David because Pedro looked at him the wrong way. On the streets, staring was a sign of disrespect called *grillin'*, and a way of testing someone's toughness. To walk away was to be a coward. Grillin' back meant not being afraid. When David grilled back at Pedro, Pedro beat him up. So David and his gang, the Crime Fam, wanted to get even.

Leo went home after the beating. His mouth was numb, and his left eye was swollen shut. His entire body ached. When his mother got home from work several hours later, Leo told her, "Mami, I got jumped." Miriam gasped at her son's bloodied face. Tears streamed down her cheeks as she picked up her purse and took her son to the hospital. Pedro went with them. Leo knew the beating was supposed to be Pedro's, but he never blamed him. What upset him more than anything was that the cops never came. Weren't they supposed to protect him? Now he didn't feel safe anymore on his own block.

Miriam concluded that it was too dangerous for Leo to attend school in the neighborhood. He received a "safety transfer," and a week later Leo took the subway about a mile north to a safer area where he would attend M.S. 20. Leo hated the new school. It reminded him of his first day at school in the United States. He was 8 years old then and even though he did not speak English, he knew his second grade classmates were making fun of him. They stole his lunch and cut in front of him in line. Leo felt so lonely he cried in the bathroom everyday and prayed that his family would move back to the Dominican Republic.

MS 20 was Leo's fourth new school in 4 years. His first class was English, followed by math, science, Spanish, social studies, and health. On his first day in the new school, Leo's health teacher discussed the circulatory system, but Leo was distracted. He was worried that the CrimeFam would be waiting for him in front of his apartment building. When the bell rang, Leo flinched. Terrified, he took the subway back to his neighborhood and shakily walked the two blocks from the train station to his apartment. He expected to be jumped, maybe this time with knives. But the only person he passed was a friend standing on the corner. Leo looked at his friend's gold and black beaded necklace. It was made of exactly 360 beads, 5 black beads alternating with 5 gold beads. Leo envied his friend. He was a member of a gang called the "Latin Kings" and didn't have to worry about getting jumped because everyone in the neighborhood respected the Kings.

* * *

When Leo visited his family in the Dominican Republic, his cousin, who had become a Latin King, invited him to join. The Kings Leo knew were always with the prettiest girls and had the best clothes. It wasn't a tough choice for Leo. Although there was no initiation in the Dominican Republic, when Leo returned to the Bronx, he had to prove himself as a King. He proudly wore his black and gold beads as he walked to his first meeting with his new Latin King brothers. He passed the broken glass window, covered with dried blood, on the stairwell of his apartment building. The window looked out onto the small patch of grass between Leo's building and the apartment building next door, where chickens fed on the garbage on the ground and the trash in a couple of abandoned shopping carts. He wasn't afraid.

When he got to the meeting, a Latin King friend introduced Leo to "El Supremo," the highest ranking Latin King in the Bronx, who greeted Leo with, "Tell me what you know about the Latin Kings." Leo was nervous. He wanted El Supremo to like him. After saying the Latin King prayer, Leo recited the basics that all Kings knew. When El Supremo asked the onlookers, what Leo had forgotten, they filled in a small omission. This error could lead to probation for Leo, a demotion in status in which his beads would be taken away or even expulsion from the gang. But El Supremo reassured Leo and told him to keep going, quizzing him on the meaning of the King colors. After responding, Leo sat quietly for a moment, and El Supremo asked if that was it. He nodded. There was a pause and Leo's heart beat faster. What if that wasn't good enough and he couldn't be a King?

El Supremo looked at Leo for what felt like an eternity, and finally said if Leo wanted to be a Latin King, he had to go to weekly meetings and memorize his lessons on the history and rules of the Kings. If he didn't know them, he would be put on probation. If he made the Latin King symbol with his hands while on probation, he'd get a beating for breaking King rules. A King only gets a beating for serious offenses like hitting a girl, going out with another King's girl, or attending a meeting drunk or high. Leo breathed a sigh of relief, happy he had chosen the Kings.

By 13, most of his friends had already joined a gang like the Latin Kings, the Bones, DDPs (Dominicans Don't Play), or AKs (All Korrupt). Leo chose the Kings for protection. And maybe it was his imagination, but every time he wore his beads, girls asked him his name followed with, "So whas' good?"

*   *   *

Leo never did technically graduate from middle school, but he was too old to repeat the eighth grade a third time. It wasn't that Leo was stupid. In fact he got the highest score in his class on a citywide practice test. He got a 52% (65% was a passing score). The problem was that Leo didn't go to class when he was bored, which happened often. Instead he'd hang out in the hallways and make out with his girlfriend.

The only time Leo went to class consistently was during basketball season. He couldn't be on the team if he failed any courses. Mr. Torres, his coach and mentor, personally promised the other teachers that he would make sure Leo, who was one of the best players, did better in their classes. Torres told his team that the real game to win in life was school. They snickered during his lectures on attacking their studies like they attacked the courts. Leo told Mr. Torres and his mom that he was going to do better in school, but also told his girlfriend that he'd meet her in the hallway whenever she asked. He didn't want to disappoint anyone.

His attendance only got worse after he learned about hooky parties. Hookies were gatherings where Leo and his friends cut school to go to someone's house to drink, dance, and have sex. His favorite hooky began at 8:30 in the morning at a friend's apartment, with Leo and several others moving the living room furniture to make space for dancing. When the buzzer rang, Leo went downstairs to let seven girls from Kennedy High School into the building. One of the girls looked at Leo and said to her friend, "He looks good with his black and gold beads." He smiled at her.

A few minutes later, another group arrived from Roosevelt High School. By 11 a.m., the apartment was packed with over 30 people. The lights were out and reggae music blasted from the stereo. Leo drank from a cup of rum as he watched several couples on the dance floor. One girl had her back against the wall and her legs wrapped around her partner's hips. He bounced her up and down in sync with the music.

A friend was lying on the floor as his dance partner straddled him and gyrated her hips. Someone asked the girl, "If I give you this condom, will you use it with him?" "*Pero claro!*" she responded ("But of course!"). Leo's friend grabbed the condom, took the girl's hand, and led her to the bedroom. Leo followed. He had hoped for a repeat of a previous party when he and two friends took turns having sex with a girl. When Leo began taking off his clothes, his friend asked, "What are you doing?" Embarrassed, Leo grabbed his clothes and left.

While sulking in the living room, some guy, whom Leo didn't know, called over to him. Leo thought, "Damn. Maybe he got beef with me." But all the guy said was, "That girl that went in there likes to have a lot of sex." A girl overheard their conversation and told Leo, "I like to have a lot of sex too." With a bashful smile, he asked, "Why don't we go in there?" When they entered the bedroom, Leo and the girl had sex on the same bed as the other couple. At some point, the couples switched partners. Leo's favorite part was when the two girls kissed each other. Earlier that morning, Leo had worried about what his mom would think if she knew he was at a hooky party. He hated the thought of disappointing her and was tempted to leave. But by the end of the party, all he could think about was his next hooky party.

A few days later, Leo saw the girl he had had sex with at the party. When he called out to her and she didn't respond, he said half jokingly, "Oh you ain't gonna look?" She turned back smugly and answered, "Do I know you?" Her words stung. Leo figured she pretended not to know him because of the way he was dressed. On the day of the hooky party, he had on his best gear, right down to the latest Michael Jordans.[1] But that day, he was wearing his old basketball clothes.

Since there was a hooky party the next day, Leo planned his outfit carefully because he assumed that she would be there. He wore his brother's Pepe jeans and his Sean John t-shirt. At that hooky party the same girl looked Leo up and down and said, "Hi, Leo." He just walked away. When she approached him again, she said, "Feel my stomach. I'm pregnant." Leo said, "Oh, yesterday you didn't know who I was and now you remember me?" He laughed at her and walked away once again.

*   *   *

Leo was supposed to go to a high school preparation program since he never graduated from eighth grade. But he slipped through the cracks and was registered as a matriculated student at Kennedy High School. He wanted to forget how many times he had gotten left behind and how some of his teachers told him he was stupid. He couldn't wait to get away from the literacy teacher who called him "a little shit" and challenged him to a fight. The only thing Leo liked about his old school was that everyone knew him—the teachers, the students, the hall monitors. Although he'd miss being popular, Leo wanted to go to school with people his own age. He just hoped that a fight with an Outlaw gang member in the neighborhood wouldn't ruin high school for him.

Leo didn't want to go alone on his first day of high school, so his brother Lisandro and his best friend Carlos went with him. When they arrived at the eight-story school building in the Bronx, they saw a line of students four city blocks long. Only one entrance was opened for the 4,600 students. They joined the line, meeting other friends along the way, and chatted. They grumbled over the length of the wait. A line-mate informed Leo that the Outlaws were always on the third floor, while most Dominicans "chilled" on the fifth floor. Someone asked Leo if he had heard about the hooky on Friday. "Nah," Leo responded. "I ain't going to hooky parties no more. I wanna do good this year." His friends laughed and one of them told him, "Nigga, everyone say that when they start high school . . . they always end up cutting. You ain't no different." Leo didn't say anything, but he was determined to prove his friends wrong.

He also figured that if high school didn't work out, he would go to Job Corps, an alternative federal residential program, where he could earn his GED and learn a trade. He learned about Job Corps 2 years earlier, when a friend on a break from the program sang its praises, telling him kids got paid for attending, the Latin Kings ruled the school, and girls had sex with the boys in the dorms.

It took more than 45 minutes to get in the door where a Kennedy staffer looked at Leo's registration papers and instructed him to go to the auditorium to get his program. He followed his friends, who navigated their way through the crowded hallways. The auditorium was equally chaotic; staff members took turns calling out student names to pick up programs. Returning students excitedly greeted each other. Leo felt out of place and told his friends, "Yo, nigga, I'm out. This is wack." They left the school and headed toward the arcades on Creston Avenue.

Leo picked up his program the next day. Trying to avoid the hallways where he had heard the Outlaws hung out, Leo managed to find his first period class and took a seat in the back, attempting not to look as uncomfortable as he felt. With heavy eyes, holding his head in his hands, Leo listened to a substitute teacher lecture for 20 minutes on the importance of getting involved in extracurricular activities. It felt like hours had passed when the bell finally rang, indicating that class was over. In the hallway, Leo heard another student boast, "No, nigga, that was me who rang the bell. Look at your watch, yo. It's only been 20 minutes." Indeed, the entire fifth floor had gotten out of class a half hour early. Leo went to his second class, which was in an uproar as boys fought for girls' attention and girls gossiped about the latest mini-dramas. The teacher walked in a few minutes later and tried to quiet the class. As soon as she turned to write something on the board, a boy threw a crumpled sheet of paper at a girl. She yelled, "Yo, I swear to God, yo." When the student told the teacher what had happened, the teacher threatened to kick anyone out who threw paper. Such disruptions were common at Kennedy.

At the conclusion of class, Leo asked the teacher where he could pick up his subway pass. She looked at his class program and pointed to his counselor's name and her room number. On the way to there, he was convinced that an Outlaw was going to jump him because of his recent fight, or that a group of Bloods might choose him as their next target. He walked nervously down the hallway until he reached room C328 and asked the woman in the cubicle closest to the entryway.

"Are you Ms. Sanchez?" The woman glared at him and pointed to the nameplate on her desk that said "Ms. Sanchez." "Don't you know how to read?" she snapped. When he asked about his subway pass card, she brusquely told him that freshmen get their applications on Friday at 9 a.m. and that he should go back to class. She turned to her computer screen without giving Leo another glance. Leo ran into a friend in the hallway, who asked if he was going to that hooky party on Friday. Leo said, "Yeah" and then left school from the girl's entrance on the first floor. It took roughly 30 minutes to walk back to the neighborhood and meet up with friends, who were also cutting school or had already dropped out.

*   *   *

By the third week into his first term of high school, Leo stopped going to school altogether. He never attended a full day at Kennedy High School. It was a Thursday in October, when the attendance counselor called Leo's home. According to her records, Leo had missed over 25 days of class. She warned Leo that if he and his mom didn't meet with her the following Monday, his mom could go to jail since she was legally responsible for his attendance.

At 8:15 on Monday morning, Leo and his mom caught the bus to Kennedy. Miriam was tired. She had gotten home from her factory job at 4 a.m. and had slept a little over 3 hours. She lectured Leo in Spanish that she had brought him to the United States for a better life and gave him everything he needed. All he had to do was go to school and study. But he didn't do anything. Leo blamed it on the school; there were too many problems. Miriam shot back, "It's because you are in a gang." "No I am not," Leo told her.

As Leo and Miriam walked from the bus stop to the school, Leo continually looked behind them to make sure they weren't being followed. He explained, "Mami, you gonna see how many security guards are in the school. A student got stabbed this summer, and now they got 80 security guards; 10 on each floor." When they entered the school, three security guards ordered Miriam and Leo to empty their pockets and put their bags through the metal detector. A security guard searched Miriam's purse while another moved a hand-held metal detector over her body.

When Leo and Miriam reached the attendance office, a counselor offered them a seat and explained that Leo had missed over 25 days of school. Miriam looked down at her shaking hands and meekly explained that she didn't know that he wasn't in school. He was always gone by the time she woke up. The counselor asked Leo what was going on. He told her there were too many problems at that school. Miriam said her son wanted to transfer to Job Corps. There was usually a 6-month waiting period, and Leo would have to go to school during that time.

Afraid that her son would not change and she'd end up in jail, Miriam asked if she could send him to the Dominican Republic during the waiting period. As long as she had a copy of the plane ticket for Leo and the address of the guardian who would take care of him in the Dominican Republic, the counselor assured her that there shouldn't be a problem.

Because Leo would have to continue going to school before leaving the country, the counselor invited Leo to eat lunch in her office instead of the cafeteria. He appreciated her offer and said, "Okay." But eating in the counselor's office would not help Leo in the hallways in-between classes when the Bloods liked to jump people. Nor would it help him on his way to school, when he could get attacked by the Outlaws. It also didn't end the chaos in his classes.

When Miriam and Leo arrived home, Leo got a 2-hour lecture:

> I don't know what to do with you anymore, Leo. Do you know
> how embarrassing it is to sit in the counselor's office and have
> the counselor ask me why my son hasn't gone to school? I
> don't know what to say. I am afraid that they won't believe me
> when I tell them that I work all night and when I wake up my
> son is gone. They make me feel like I'm a bad parent. When
> the school calls, I tell them, "No, my son is not at home. He
> is in school." It makes me sad to send you to the Dominican
> Republic because there is nothing there. People are so poor that
> they fight just to eat. And you have all the opportunities in the
> world and you don't do anything.

With Leo sprawled on the couch, his arm covering his eyes, Miriam cried, frustrated and desperate to make her son understand what she was saying. She continued,

> I came to this country so that you could have a better life.
> When I was in school, I used to split the pages in my notebook
> in half so I could use every part of them because I knew how
> much my family sacrificed to buy them. You use one page and
> throw it away. You don't understand that they cost money. I
> want you to have a better life. I have to work in a factory be-

cause I don't speak English. I work the worst hours in the worst places and get the worst pay because those are the only jobs I can get. I get treated like an animal, like a rat. I want you to have a better life. But I don't see a future for you. Maybe selling drugs or robbing people or going to jail because you don't like to work and you don't go to school, so how are you going to support yourself?

Leo responded, "Mami, I'll go to school." Tired of his promises, she continued, "I have gotten so many letters and phone calls from your schools. You always say that you are going to change, but nothing changes. . . ." Leo went to his room and his mom sat on the couch, feeling defeated; when she felt the migraine begin she got ready for work.

*   *   *

Miriam officially withdrew Leo from Kennedy High School and bought his ticket to the Dominican Republic with money she borrowed from her brother. Before he left, Leo signed up for Job Corps and was placed on the 3- to 6-month waiting list. He left New York City on November 25, 2003. Excluding two summer visits, it had been 8 years since Leo lived in the Dominican Republic.

Leo stayed at his grandma's house where his favorite uncle, Radhame, and three cousins lived. His aunt and two other cousins lived two doors away. At first Leo didn't like living in the Dominican Republic (DR). In the Bronx, he was rarely at home. But in the DR, anytime Leo went outside, 5 minutes later his Grandma or Uncle Radhame went looking for him. It drove Leo crazy. "My grandma think she slick," Leo told a friend. A few nights earlier, he was flirting with a girl in the street when his Grandma told him his mom was on the phone. Leo ran home and when he picked up the telephone, no one was on the other line. He was about to go outside when his grandma insisted he stay home because it was too late to go out. When Leo accused her of lying about the phone call, she simply told him to go to sleep.

Even though Teresa was strict with Leo, they had a good relationship. Leo liked joking around with his grandma and sometimes he'd give her such a big hug that he'd practically lift her off the ground. She'd "shoo" him away laughing, which only made him hug her more. For a 65-year-old Grandma with 10 grandchildren, she was a spitfire. Teresa, or Teri as her family and neighbors called her, was happiest when she was taking care of her family. A large extended family meant there was always something to do and prevented her from being lazy, a trait she detested. She was proud not to be the type of woman to stop working just because her kids sent her money from the United States. It was important to Teresa to pay her own bills.

At the same time, Teresa was thankful that her house had been refurbished thanks to the money Leo's Uncle Siso had sent from the United States. The family had added on a *colmado* since Leo had last lived in DR. (A *colmado* is a windowless Dominican version of a New York bodega, where neighbors can buy basic household products, fruits, and vegetables.) Leo spent most of his time in the Dominican Republic in front of that colmado with his grandmother, his cousins, and his father. Leo never really knew his father before that visit. They had only lived together for a couple of years, and his father wasn't around much then. But when Moreno found out that Leo was moving back for a few months because he was having trouble in school, he rented a decrepit one-room wooden house a block away from Teresa's house. Every day, he picked Leo up and took him to work, fixing car tires. At night, they'd hang out in front of the colmado. Leo and Moreno talked about everything. School, girls, hooky parties, Moreno's adventures in the United States—everything. He told Leo about his half sister, the little girl Maholi had met years earlier in the supermarket. Moreno knew his son was a "player," and he didn't want the two to meet and have sex without knowing they were related. He gave his son her phone number and Leo promised to call when he returned. Moreno gave Leo fatherly advice like, "Stay in school. Work hard."

But what Leo really liked about his father was that he knew how to have fun. Moreno knew everyone. He'd slowly drive down the street waving to friends from his car as if he were a celebrity. He'd stop along the way, telling Leo to buy beer and bring enough cups for as many people as there were in the car. When one of the pretty young neighbors wanted to mess around with Leo, he took her to his father's house because he knew his dad would understand. Moreno happily gave them privacy and told his son, "Go have babies. Make me grandchildren. I'll take care of them." Leo and Moreno were more like friends than father and son. By the end of that trip, he was Leo's favorite relative in the Dominican Republic.

When Leo wasn't with his father, he was usually with his friends and cousins. Everyone wanted to hear what Nueva York was really like. Was it true that you could get a job making $500 a week? Ruddy, Leo's oldest cousin, was particularly interested in working in the United States. Since he was 14 and his father was killed in a bar fight, he'd taken care of his grandma, mom, and three siblings. What Ruddy wanted was to give his family whatever they needed—a nice house, a car—to be able to buy a new shirt and pants in the same month. His family marveled at all the books he read on how to get rich. His favorite was *The 21 Most Important Minutes in a Leader's Day*. Ruddy enrolled in a business program at the local university, but he dropped out when his friend introduced him to a money-making pyramid scheme. After 6 months, he hadn't made a dime, but was convinced he was about to hit it big. In the meantime, Ruddy ran the family *colmado,* earning $15 a day. He wanted to go to New York and get as many jobs as possible to save money for a house. For Ruddy, New York was the most likely ticket to financial success because the only people he knew, who had improved their lives financially, were business owners or people who had lived in New York.

*   *   *

Leo had been in the Dominican Republic for almost 3 months when his mom phoned to say that Job Corps had called, and he was to start school the following week. Miriam couldn't wait to see Leo. She missed him terribly. He was on a plane back to New York a week later and on a bus the following Monday to Delaware Valley Job Corps Center, a few hours outside of New York City. Leo was convinced that if he were in a place where he didn't have to worry about "beef," then he would do well in school. His plan was to get his GED and learn to fix cars so he could get a job and make money. Excited about his future, he was determined to make his family proud.

8

Leo's Girlfriend, Ana

Leo in the Dominican Republic, a week before starting Job Corps

I didn't mean to slap her. . . . Sometimes I get mad and act different to ruff I don't know why . . . sometimes I hit her hard but I never mean to touch her. . . . I be thinking to leave her to break up with her but I think I can't be living without her even though I don't like her telling me what to. I going to miss that.

Leo's Diary, Winter 2005

L EO SAT ON A CHAIR in the Job Corps recreation room as a friend
braided his hair into tight zigzagging rows across his head. Some
girl whom Leo didn't know greeted them on her way out the door
to smoke a cigarette. Leo warned her, "Smoking's bad for you." But she
ignored him and walked away. Leo's friend told him, "That's Ana, and
she like you." Although she wasn't his type, Leo liked the idea of being
liked. When the girl finished braiding Leo's hair, she ran off to find Ana
and informed her, "What you think of Leo? He like you."

In the end, Ana approached Leo. He greeted her with, "What's pop-
pin'?" She could tell right away that he was a player. He licked his lips
seductively as he looked her up and down. Ana asked, "Where you
from?" Leo responded, "The Bronx." "Where?" she asked. "Creston
and 182nd Street." "I'm from 176th and Tremont." She was a neighbor,
but Leo thought her neighborhood was even rougher than his. Plus he
had beef with some of the "Morenos" (Blacks) there.

The first time they met, Leo had been at the Job Corps for 3 weeks
and Ana for 14 months. She was 17 years old and Leo was 16, but lied
and told her he was 17 too. Ana was in the word processing and hotel
program, wanted to go to college, get a good job, and was determined
not to "be dependent on nobody."

She thought Leo was too skinny, but liked that he was about a foot
taller than her, had long thick lashes and braids. They talked until
the 9:30 curfew when Leo walked Ana back to her dorm. Leo pulled
her to the side of the building and asked her for a kiss. Ana didn't say
anything. She almost told him that she already had a man, but decided against it. They talked a few more minutes and Leo said, "I'm
cold, yo. I only got this sweater. If you kiss me, then I won't be cold."
Ana thought about resisting as he leaned down to kiss her. That kiss
marked the beginning of their relationship.

Leo picked Ana up every day in front of her dorm, so they could eat
breakfast together. He waited for her in-between classes, and they talked
for hours after dinner. Leo listened attentively when she told him about
her violent family. Ana applied to the Job Corps to escape the abuse at
home. "My dad used to beat me, and I didn't want to take it no more.
So I came to Job Corps." She resented her mom for all of the times she
watched her father beat her without trying to stop him. "The only thing
my mom cares about is her man." Ana recalled how her dad told her that
she was stupid and that he wished she had never been born.

She had a reputation at the Job Corps for being tough. Leo was
warned that Ana is bad news. "She fight everybody." She had an explo-
sive temper, and when she lost control, she would scream and swear,
with fists up, ready to fight. Leo didn't care. He fell hard for Ana.

* * *

During their first 2 months together, they were inseparable. After classes Ana taught Leo how to type in the computer room. After dinner they hung out in the recreation room. When Leo thought about quitting the Job Corps, Ana was the one who encouraged him to stay. And when Ana passed her pre-GED exam, no one was more proud of her than Leo. Ana shared helpful hints with Leo about the Job Corps, like the best places to hide from staff members and how to break curfew without getting caught. Leo became an expert at sneaking out of Ana's dorm window, which earned him the nickname Robin Hood among his friends.

The first sign of trouble began 2 months into their relationship when a mutual friend told Ana that Leo had been talking to a girl who was notorious for having sex at hooky parties. When Ana found Leo in the hallway, he asked, "What happened?" He could tell something was wrong by the expression on her face. With her arms crossed, she responded, "I heard you be talking to that girl that have sex with everybody at hookies." "What?" Leo asked in a surprised voice. She repeated slowly and with more emphasis, "I heard you be talking with that girl and I wanna know if it's true." "What the fuck are you talking about?" Leo responded. It was true that Leo had talked to that girl, but he would never disrespect Ana by doing something with her. Leo was so angry that he walked away. They made up, but only after Ana begged Leo to forgive her.

Ana became painfully suspicious and jealous of other girls. Maybe it stemmed from her own infidelity. She had previously taken revealing pictures of herself and gave half to Leo and half to an ex-boyfriend Leo never knew about. Regardless of the reason, whenever Leo went home on the weekends, she'd ask mutual friends, "You see Leo this weekend at any parties? He be with any girls?" Most weekends he stayed in his house. But if the opportunity to mess with an attractive girl came up, he took advantage of it. One weekend, Ana came home with Leo. He purposely started a fight with her so that she would leave his apartment because friends promised to bring some girls over. Ana would test Leo, "I know you been messing with other girls." Normally Leo would just tell Ana to shut up, but one day he lost his temper and slapped her face. She looked at Leo in horror and ran off crying. Leo felt bad and again they made up. A series of fights and make-ups followed.

* * *

The Job Corps wasn't what Leo had expected and by summer, he hated it. During orientation the staff had laid out strict rules—no drugs, no drinking, no fighting, and no gang activity. This was the environment Leo was hoping for. But the reality was that gang fights were incessant and drugs were so accessible that one of Leo's roommates smoked weed every night. One student ended up in the hospital from an overdose. But the biggest problem at the school was that Leo didn't feel safe. Older students glared at him. He worried about getting jumped while playing basketball in the gym. By the end of the first month, he walked outside with a makeshift weapon, a pool ball hidden in a sock. One of the "Morenos" (Blacks) had jumped a Latino, and the Latinos wanted revenge. Leo didn't want to fight, but he was afraid that if he didn't join in, then no one would help him in the future if he ever had trouble. The fight never happened, but Leo found himself facing the same problems he had hoped to get away from. The only difference between the Job Corps and the Bronx was that the Job Corps felt like prison. Leo could not leave when he wanted, the food was bad, and he had a curfew.

The other big disappointment was that the school cut his trade program. During the first month of classes, Leo learned how to fix the exterior of cars. He attended all of his classes, even the academic classes that he found boring. But when the auto body teacher left the Job Corps, they switched him to a different program that he did not like. Leo lost interest in his classes and started coming home every weekend. When his mom asked about school, he said he liked it so she wouldn't worry. Leo's counselor predicted that the fastest he could pass the GED test would be in 2 years, but that was only if he began to study outside of class time, and if he took advantage of the tutoring sessions. Many days Leo slept through his classes and never went to tutoring. Trouble with other students continued, and when one of them threw a sock full of feces on his bed, he quit Job Corps. Ana sadly walked Leo to the bus back to the city. He looked down at Ana and spoke in a paternal voice, "You gotta study so you pass the GED and go to college." "I know," she responded, pleased at Leo's attention. They hugged and kissed goodbye with promises to talk on the phone. Leo didn't want to leave Ana and his friends, but he couldn't wait to get out of the Job Corps. His plan was to get a job and enroll in a GED class.

* * *

When Leo arrived in the Bronx, he dropped his suitcase in his room and went to find his friends, who filled him in on the latest gossip. Someone had beef with the Bloods because one of them had been stabbed and now they were looking for the Blood. One friend was going to be a father, and another was working at a clothing store downtown called VIP. Leo pleaded with him, "Can you get me a job there? I need a job, yo." His friend promised to get Leo an application and put in a good word for him.

After a month, Leo still hadn't heard from the clothing store. He had filled out the application, leaving the "Education" and "Work experience" sections largely blank. He decided to make an appointment with a Job Corps counselor to help him find GED classes. But the counselor only knew of classes an hour away by car. Leo didn't bother taking the entrance exam. He knew there was no way he would attend a program so far away. One of his friends from the Job Corps claimed to have bought a GED diploma for $300. So Leo's new plan was to buy one for himself. All he had to do was find out where and how. But no one seemed to know. Leo's second and third months home were similar to the first. He tried to stay away from trouble by sleeping in, watching television, and hanging out with his *tranquilo* friends, like Carlos.

* * *

In the meantime, Ana was still at the Job Corps, but was tired of the classes and wanted to quit. She was sick of the rules and the gossip among students. The classes were boring and she couldn't grasp English grammar, no matter how hard she studied, usually no more than a few minutes a day. She was even more discouraged after taking a GED practice test and failing by nine points. Ana set deadlines. "If I don't pass my practice test by September, then I am going to quit."

Leo encouraged her to leave. "Job Corps is wack," he told her in a phone call. "Why you wanna stay there? Move to New York and I can rent an apartment so we can live together" he advised her. His offer was tempting. Ana missed Leo desperately, regardless of their arguments and jealous spats. If they lived together, she could also make sure that he wasn't "messing" with other girls. She had doubts though. Leo only had a part-time job that paid minimum wage, so how was he going to get a place for both of them?

The next day Ana told her counselor she planned to move to New York. The counselor feared she'd end up back at her parents' house and her father would beat her. She asked Ana how she'd get a job without a high school diploma and warned her how hard it was to find a job that pays more than minimum wage. She also encouraged Ana to think about how close she was to passing and how hard she had worked. Ana listened unenthusiastically and said, "I'll stay until December and if I don't pass by then, I'll quit." By the end of their conversation, Ana walked out of her counselor's office once again determined to get her GED and go to college. She wasn't going to let anything get in her way. Ana returned to her afternoon classes and stared off into space as the instructor gave a grammar lesson. The gossip continued. Friends talked behind her back and rumors about Leo's infidelity spread. Ana quit the Job Corps in December, 5 months after Leo.

* * *

When Ana moved to the city, she shared a two-bedroom apartment just north of the Bronx with 13 other people. Her room was one of the closets. Leo's mom suggested that Ana move in with them and get a job to help pay rent. Ana unpacked her two backpacks and hung her clothes in Leo's closet. She promised Miriam that she would start looking for a job the next day. Ana had every intention of getting up early and filling out job applications, but she'd end up watching television until 4 or 5 in the morning. Her job search turned into telling friends, "I need to find a job, yo. Help me find a job." But no one knew of any jobs. Instead of contributing to the household, Ana became another mouth to feed.

Living together was disastrous for Leo and Ana's relationship. Ana would eavesdrop on Leo's phone conversations. She asked friends where Leo had been and who he was with. A friend, who lived upstairs, gladly kept an eye on Leo. When Ana told Leo about the rumors she had heard, he either brushed off the accusations or told her to shut up. Leo was equally suspicious of Ana, but instead of spying on her, he kept her in the apartment as much as possible. One day Ana got ready to go outside and meet a friend. Leo asked where she was going. She anxiously responded, "With Kara." "I don't want you hanging out with her. She's a ho. You have to stay here with Maholi." Ana obeyed, and when Leo got ready to go out, she'd offer to go with him. "You have to stay here with Maholi." She watched him put lotion on his face and check himself in the mirror before walking out the door.

When he returned hours later, Ana asked, "Where were you? You been to a hooky party? You better not be messing with other girls." Leo was angered by her accusations.

One time Ana found a videotape of Leo dancing with a girl at a hooky party. She was infuriated when she saw him trying to pull down the girl's jeans to take a picture of her thong. Their fights escalated from shouting to hitting. One night Ana got mouthy with Leo in front of his friends, so he slapped her. Juan Carlos got up from the couch and scolded Leo, "Yo, that ain't right. You can't hit a girl." With that Leo left.

Ana sometimes got physical too. When she caught Leo at a hooky party, she marched up to him and slapped him across the face. A bunch of Leo's friends were about to jump her, but Leo stood in front of her and said "If anyone touches her, I hit you. That's my girl." Ana swelled with pride. When she was really mad at him, she would tell Leo that she had been with other guys. "Don't you know that every time you eat me out you smell another nigga?" When Leo and Ana would make up, she'd confess that she had not been with other guys. As proof she'd affirm, "You know if I be with another guy 'cuz my hole be bigger. I'd feel different." They got back together until another argument led to another breakup.

One day, Ana was about to take a shower when she remembered something she needed. She opened the door to find Miriam's boyfriend in the doorway. He walked away as if nothing had happened. But Ana was convinced that he had been spying on her and ran to Maholi's room to tell her what happened. When she couldn't stop crying, Maholi called Leo and Lisandro, who were upstairs at their friend Pedro's apartment. Leo was so angry he called his Uncle Siso, who called Leo's mom and told her off for allowing "that bum" to stay in their apartment. Leo's mom believed her boyfriend, who denied the accusation, and forbid Ana to be in the apartment when she wasn't there. Ana decided, "I can't stay here. I don't want that nigga staring at me."

* * *

She moved in with a friend that night, two blocks from Leo's apartment. Ana was homeless again a month later when they got evicted for not paying rent. She told Leo that she was scared to be on the streets alone, so he promised to stay with her. For 4 nights they stayed in the Kentucky Fried Chicken, until it closed at 4 in the morning. They roamed the streets until Leo's mom and boyfriend left for work at 11 a.m. Leo and Ana slept on the couch, making sure they left before any-one came home.

Leo asked Pedro if Ana could rent a room in his apartment. The move would be temporary until Ana found a job and a place to stay. The friend's older sister worked in a club in Connecticut and told Ana, "On a good night you can make up to $100. All you got to do is dance or have a drink with whatever nigga come up to you. You could work there too." The easy money was appealing to Ana, but Leo refused to let her work there. He worried how it would look that his girl got paid for hanging out with other guys. Needing money, Leo changed his mind under the condition that she tell people that she cleaned office buildings. Once Ana started earning more money than Leo, he'd ask, "Ana, lend me $20." Even if she was late with her $65 weekly rent, she never refused Leo's requests. "I love him, so of course I put him first."

Ana liked making money, but she complained, "Niggas dance with you and they get big, you know what I am saying. Sometimes I stop dancing with them because I can feel them up on me." Ana had only planned on working at the club until she found another job. She wanted a job that respected her mind. "Niggas dance with you because you got a nice body, not because you are smart, you know what I'm saying?" But 1 month turned into 2 and 2 months turned into 3. She worried that she would get stuck there like some of the other girls. One girl started working at the club when she was 15 years old. She was now 20. That same girl had a room off of 174th Street and Crotona and was looking for a roommate. Ana rented the room, but her fights with Leo almost cost her the apartment.

One night Ana threw a party for her roommate. The eight friends attending were listening to the music Lisandro had downloaded from the Internet onto his laptop. Ana was mad at Leo and told him that she wanted to talk to him. He snapped back, "No!" With that she slammed the laptop shut and started to walk away. Leo grabbed her and slapped her in the face. He hit her again and again, until finally Ana's room-mate got between them and told Leo to stop. He grabbed the laptop and stormed out of the window and down the fire escape. Leo had hit her before, but never in front of all of her friends. She felt humiliated and told herself that this time they were done.

Her roommate threatened to kick her out because she had been in abusive relationships in the past and didn't want anything to do with them. Ana begged her to let her stay and promised it wouldn't happen again because she and Leo were over. But when Leo came back later that night and asked to talk with Ana, she went without much coaxing. Leo told her that he blacked out and lost control. He felt horrible. By the end of the conversation they were back together, and Ana concluded that she must really love Leo because after everything that had happened, she still wanted to be with him.

* * *

Leo was noticeably sweeter toward Ana right up until leaving for the Dominican Republic to visit his family. During the 6 weeks that he was away, Ana started dating a guy from work. He was a 24-year-old Mexican lumberer, who rented a room in White Plains, a suburb north of the Bronx. Ana didn't tell Leo about him until he returned to New York. She rationalized, "At least I told Leo that I be playing him. When he play me, he try to hide it." Leo hit Ana and demanded that she quit her job and be with him exclusively. "How am I gonna pay rent if I quit my job?" she challenged. "I'll pay for it," he promised.

Ana quit her job and left the Mexican after a month of going back and forth between the two men. Leo paid Ana's first month's rent of $190 for a room at Leo's friend's apartment.[1] But by the second month, he realized that renting that room was a bad idea. Unlike his own mom, his friend's mom, who rented the room to him, never cooked and was always arguing with him. Plus, her son and his friends smoked so much weed that it stunk up the entire apartment.

As an escape, Leo started going to hooky parties again. He left the apartment with promises of going to work or to look for a job, but would return drunk at 4 or 5 a.m. Ana grumbled, "One time he came home at 9 in the morning. You gonna tell me that he's not with other girls?"

The smoke in the apartment didn't become a serious problem until Ana found out she was pregnant. Initially, Leo was excited to have a child. He called all of his friends and told them the good news. But the novelty wore off when Ana began throwing up. He complained, "I get money to buy her food and then she says that she don't want it or she throws it up. She be throwing up too much. Something wrong with her." It wasn't the throwing up that really bothered Leo, but the fact that he didn't really know if he was the father. Regardless of his doubts, Leo took Ana to the hospital and waited all afternoon only to be told that her "morning sickness" was normal.

Leo didn't think that having a baby would change his life very much. He figured that he'd take care of the baby during the day and Ana would take care of it at night.

* * *

For financial support, Leo was counting on the money from Ana's lawsuit. Her family was suing their former landlord for lead poisoning. Her current lawyer estimated that she could win as much as $500,000 because of the high levels of lead in her blood. Level 10 was considered lead poisoning. The Department of Health got involved at levels 15 or above. Ana's blood level was 36.

While Ana waited for her case to be tried, Leo was content taking food from his mom's house to feed her. Ana, on the other hand, thought, "He's my man and he supposed to take care of me." What Ana didn't know was that whatever food he had, he gave to her. The only time he ate was at Juan Carlos's apartment. When he didn't go there, he didn't eat. He never told her that, no matter how much she complained, because he didn't want her to worry.

Ana spent most of her days sitting in her room obsessing about Leo. She was always angry at him for something, whether it was paying rent late, going to hooky parties, or having to wait for him to bring her food. It hurt Leo every time she told him that he was lazy. From his perspective, "At least I always try my best to see her eat and whenever she gets mad, I always try to get whatever she want."

Ana gave Leo an ultimatum. He had a month to change. If he didn't, then she would get an abortion. She didn't want one, but she worried about supporting a child when she could barely take care of herself. After finding out that she was 5 months pregnant, she made up her mind. "I ain't got no belly. If I have that baby, it would come out with problems 'cuz it don't weigh nothing."

Ana went downtown to a Planned Parenthood clinic where she began a 2-day abortion process. The second day, Leo took Ana to her doctor's appointment, but when he realized she was there for an abortion, he left. He couldn't forgive her for killing his baby.

Ana came home from the doctor's and watched Spanish soap operas, waiting for Leo to bring her food. He handed her a bag of Chinese takeout and asked, "How can you murder my son?" "Oh, now he's your son?" Ana snapped back. She was still bitter from Leo's accusation earlier that week that she didn't know who the father was. Even though it was true, she was infuriated that he disrespected her that way in front of his sister. Plus, Ana was almost certain that the baby was Leo's. She never used protection with Leo, and always used protection with her ex-boyfriend. Ana threw a glass at Leo, screaming that she had warned him about the abortion if he didn't change. It missed Leo and shattered against the wall, cutting Ana. Blood gushed from her hand as Leo stormed out. Ana started to cry. "The fucking asshole left me sitting here with my hand bleeding."

Ana decided that she had to move because she didn't want Leo staying with her anymore. A friend from Job Corps said that she could stay in her apartment because her mom was in the Dominican Republic for the winter.

* * *

A few days later, Leo had some girls at his mom's apartment. Knowing this, his sister brought Ana to the apartment. When they walked in, the lights were out, Spanish music was playing, and empty Corona beer bottles were on the floor. What had started out as an intimate gathering turned into a full-blown hooky party. Ana looked at Leo, turned around and walked out. Leo was so mad at his sister for bringing Ana that he smacked her in the face. She grabbed an empty bottle to hit Leo. Juan Carlos took it away from her and told Maholi, "Chill." She went to the kitchen and got a knife. Juan Carlos laughed and said, "What are you going to do with that?" She lunged at Leo, but Juan Carlos grabbed her arm and twisted it behind her back, forcing her to drop the knife. He pushed her to the couch and yelled, "Chill!" Maholi walked out and came back a few minutes later with the police. They handcuffed Leo and were about to take him away when he told them that his sister went after him with a knife. When the police threatened, "If one goes to the station, you both go," Maholi dropped the charges.

When Leo's mom found out about the party, she hit Leo in the shin with a cane and screamed, "What do you think this is!" She followed Leo as he walked out the door. Juan Carlos was in the hallway, and she told him that Leo didn't live there anymore. Leo spent the next couple of nights at Juan Carlos's house. When he came home Sunday, his mom had his suitcase packed and told him that he had until Friday to either get a job or go back to school. Nothing changed, and 2 weeks later Leo's mom left him alone in the apartment when she and Maholi went to the Dominican Republic for New Year's. Leo gave Juan Carlos an extra set of keys, and he walked into Leo's apartment one night to find the Christmas tree in shambles on the floor next to the television. "What the fuck," Juan Carlos yelled. It looked as if the apartment had been ransacked. He found Ana on top of Leo, choking him. Leo pushed her off. She got up, but Leo tripped her. She stumbled and was about to go after Leo again when Juan Carlos carried her to the kitchen. Ana was drunk, but in Juan Carlos's opinion, she was acting crazy, almost possessed. Ana screamed, "He's not staying here. Get the fuck out. I'm the only one staying here tonight." Leo gave Ana money for a cab, but she threw it on the floor, and insisted that she sleep at Leo's apartment. Juan Carlos eventually got Ana downstairs and put her in a cab.

The next day Ana woke up with a bad hangover and a fat lip. She refused to take Leo's phone calls. Leo stopped by almost every day until Ana talked to him again. A friend suggested they see a counselor. Leo was willing, but Ana wasn't.

A few days later, Leo called Ana and her roommate told him that Ana wasn't there. Leo assumed she was really there but didn't want to talk to him. When Ana came over later that night, he asked her, "Where were you today?" "I was home all day," she said in an annoyed voice. He slapped her and Ana cried as she pleaded with Leo to believe her. Leo apologized later, "I didn't mean to slap her. . . I never mean to touch her, but she do stuff that make me hit her like coming to my house and breaking everything. Sometime I wish she could take counseling because honestly she don't act normal. I be thinking to leave her. To break up with her, but I think I can't be living without her. Even though I don't like her telling me what to do I going to miss that!"

When Leo called Ana a few days later, her roommate told him, "Come pick up your girl before I fuck her up." Leo thought she was joking until he went to the apartment to find Ana's bags in front of the door.

He went downstairs to Ana's cousin's apartment. Ana answered the door crying and told Leo, "I'm sorry, Leo, but she said you stole $7, so I punched her." With nowhere to go, Ana was afraid of being on the streets again. Leo assured her that he would take care of her. That night Ana and Leo slept on the stairway leading to the roof in his building. But Ana was freezing and she couldn't stop crying. So Leo finally told her that they were going to his apartment. Ana refused, scared that his mom would kick them both out. They sneaked into his bed, and he watched Ana drift to sleep. Leo stayed up all night to make sure Ana was out of the apartment before his mom saw her. Ana moved into her cousin's home and became the live-in babysitter.

*   *   *

Ana's lead poisoning case was finally being tried. Her lawyer's biggest priority was getting her parents to cooperate. The last time her parents visited the office, Ana's father demanded money and accused the lawyer of stealing from him. He threatened to hire another lawyer before storming out. Since that meeting, Ana's mother had not shown up for any of the appointments. In order to win the case, they needed her mom to testify about previous doctor's visits and complaints to the landlord about peeling paint. Ana said she would talk to her sister, who would talk to her mom. Ana hadn't talked to her parents in years, which was why she met alone with their lawyer.

The lawyer prepped Ana for court. He told her how to dress and role-played some of the questions that the other lawyer might ask her. The case started the following Monday and lasted 2 weeks. Ana's mom decided to participate and was the first of their family to testify. Ana did the same several days later, and the lawyer assured her that she did very well. On the final day of the trial, the judge asked the jury if they reached a verdict. After 10 years of waiting, Ana lost her case.

The lawyers promised Ana that they would appeal with a good chance of winning. In the meantime, Ana wanted to go back to school. She applied to Interboro College where she could get her GED and take college courses at the same time. When Ana filled out the financial aid application, she realized that she needed her parents' signature. They refused. School would have to wait. Ana ended up getting a filing job in an office through her cousin's wife. But after her 2nd week, her boss fired her.

* * *

Ana and Leo hadn't spoken much since she moved to her cousin's apartment. He prohibited Ana from talking to Leo if she wanted to live with him. He even changed the phone number so Leo couldn't call. But after a few days of not talking, Ana would miss Leo and call him when her cousin and his wife weren't home.

Leo was supposed to call Ana one day, but he didn't. When Lisandro's girlfriend, Betty, told her that he didn't call because he had been with another girl, Ana flipped. She got revenge by giving her number to a guy at a party she went to with Leo, Lisandro, and Betty. Lisandro told Leo what he saw. He got so mad at Ana for disrespecting him that he started hitting her. When Ana went home later that night with bruises, her cousin told her that if she spoke to Leo again, she would have to move out. After several days of begging and pleading, Leo finally convinced her to go to his apartment so that they could talk. They made up, and when her cousin found out, Ana was homeless again.

Leo once again promised to take care of her and found a room for Ana to rent. Leo scrounged up $300, mostly borrowed from friends, and paid Ana's first month of rent. She found a job at a clothing store on Fordham Road, but didn't think she would stay long. She didn't like that manager. When rent was next due, Ana couldn't pay it. Neither could Leo. Ana cursed at him and accused him of never keeping his promises. That was it. Leo was done with Ana. When Ana was forced to go to a homeless shelter, she swore she would never speak to Leo again.

What Ana hated most about living in the shelter were the rules. She had to be in by 9:30 at night and out by 8 in the morning. There was no drinking and no drugs. They checked her purse whenever she entered the shelter. Ana wanted to get a job so she could move out as soon as possible. But the bigger motivator was to prove to Leo that she didn't need him anymore. She ended up working at a Burger King earning $6.00 an hour. It would be a month before she got her first pay check.

Ana entertained herself by talking with her new boyfriend, the security guard at the clinic where she received free counseling. He was older, and even though he was still living with his mom, Ana thought he was better than Leo because at least he had a job. When they started dating, Ana made sure to tell Betty about him, hoping it would get back to Leo. She bragged about how much better her life was without Leo. But she eventually broke up with her new boyfriend because he never had time for her. Leo had always had time for Ana. Even though she missed him, Ana refused to call Leo. Instead she turned to Betty for news about Leo, calling her at least once a week, "just to talk."

Ana moved out of the shelter when her brother asked her to move in with him. She got a second job at a restaurant and hoped to save enough money to find her own place. Things were looking up until Ana's brother told her that her parents were on the verge of being evicted. He insisted that Ana help them, so she gave them her entire $300 check, leaving her with nothing. When Ana dropped off the money, her father yelled at her for not having more money. She swore that she would have nothing more to do with them.

When she went back to her brother's apartment, he suggested she move in with their parents and give her paychecks to them until they got more money. Ana thought he was crazy. She refused to move.

What Ana really wanted to do was talk to Leo. They hadn't spoken in almost 3 months, but she still thought about him, still missed him. She wondered if he missed her too.

9

Leo's Sister, Maholi

The family house under construction in the Dominican Republic

Ten years from now . . . I see myself helping my family, especially my mom and my little sister because they are both women. . . . My sister has to graduate. Even if I don't graduate, she has to because I will make sure of it.
Leo, conversation, 2001

EVERYONE CALLED HER MAHOLI. But that was a nickname, which came from a Spanish soap opera character. Relatives couldn't remember the reason for the name, attributing it most often to a similar stutter or skin color as the soap opera character. Two years younger than Leo, Maholi sometimes got so excited when she spoke that her words toppled over one another, mixed in with giggles. Even though Maholi and Leo fought almost every day, Maholi felt that her brother really understood her. Leo felt it was his duty to make sure she graduated from high school.

Maholi was traditionally the most obedient of the three siblings. When her mom told her to do something, she listened. If her mom set a curfew, Maholi obeyed. When Leo and Lisandro told her to do something, usually the chores that they were assigned, she did them. This is the story of when she didn't.

*   *   *

Maholi was late for high school one very snowy day. Annoyed that she had lost her subway pass, she grabbed her book bag, put on a jacket, and slipped a blade into her pocket. By the time she reached her school, she was soaking wet and very late for class. The truancy truck drove by, and the officer asked for her school program. When he checked her pockets and found the blade, he took her to the security office. She thought about telling the truth, but instead said that she used the knife to open boxes at her grocery store job. They didn't believe her and suspended her from school. Maholi was given a hearing date and told to bring her mom when she came back.

Maholi didn't want her mom to know what happened, so she called her cousin and asked that she go instead. After much begging and pleading, her cousin finally agreed. The next day Maholi woke up, got dressed and left by 7:45, just like any other school day. But instead of going to school, she spent the day at her friend's apartment. Her mom never knew she had been suspended.

A few days before the school hearing, her cousin called and told her she couldn't go to her school because "something came up." Desperate to find an adult to go to the hearing, Maholi called a family friend and explained that she took the blade for protection. Someone had already gotten stabbed at school, and she didn't want to be the next victim. But if she told the teachers, they'd try to find the attackers. Then Maholi would really have problems because they'd seek revenge. Her friend suggested that she tell her mom. Maholi was convinced that if she did, her mom would send her back to the Dominican Republic. But if she didn't go to the meeting with her mom, the school would kick her out. Maholi explained, "I like my school yo. I don't want to leave my school. Sometimes I skip classes but its only to get food cuz that cafeteria food is nasty, yo." When her friend laughed, Maholi justified, "You can't get in the way of a fat girl and her food." At 14 years old, Maholi was 5 feet 10 inches tall and weighed around 180 pounds. Because she was not allowed to go out when her mom was not home, Maholi treated her boredom with food. Her high school friends nicknamed her "Gorda," fat girl.

The family friend refused to go to the hearing with Maholi. So Maholi pleaded with the dean to let her have her hearing without her mom. He agreed since she said her mom was in the hospital for migraine headaches. Maholi was sent temporarily to a school for youth at risk of violent behavior. She completed the week-long program and went back in her regular classes at Jane Addams High School. Her mom never found out that she had been suspended for bringing a weapon to school.

★   ★   ★

The next sign of trouble began when Maholi's friend called and told Lisandro that Maholi had been buying a lot of stuff lately with a credit card. Lisandro ignored the warning, annoyed that this guy was butting into his business. A few weeks later, Lisandro found Maholi counting money on their mom's bed. "What happened?" he asked, assuming there was a reason she had so much money. "Mami told me to take out $20," she said awkwardly. Lisandro didn't think anything of it, but when he called his mom later that day and mentioned the $20, she said that she never told Maholi to take out that money. When Lisandro confronted her, she grabbed as much money as she could from her mom's coat pockets and walked out the door. Leo had once blackened Maholi's eye for lying. This was much worse. She had been taking money out of her mom's bank account for a few months. So she decided to run away.

Miriam came home around 11 p.m. After 8 hours of cleaning airplane bathrooms at JFK airport and commuting 5 hours to and from work, Miriam was exhausted. Bone weary, she unlocked the door to the apartment and asked, "Where's Maholi?" When Leo told her that she was out, Miriam curled up on the couch and waited for her daughter to return. When she woke up and realized Maholi still wasn't home, she walked over to her leather coat. After looking in the pocket, she cried, "*Dios mio!*" Miriam had taken $10,000 from her savings account for a trip to the Dominican Republic. She had been saving money ever since she came to the United States. Years of pinching pennies; years of working 12-hour days at minimum wages, all so that she could finish building her house in the Dominican Republic. She had already used most of her savings to build the foundation. That $10,000 was all she needed to complete her home. And now the $10,000 was gone. Miriam sobbed.

Maholi didn't come home that night. The next morning Miriam went to her bank. She was supposed to have around $2,000 in her checking account, but there was only $500. Leo, Lisandro, and Miriam took a cab to Maholi's school. When they arrived, Leo touched his mom's shoulder and pointed, "Mami, look, there's Maholi." Lisandro had gotten a security guard from the school in case she tried to run. Instead, she got into a cab with her family, and they went home.

Miriam asked Maholi over and over again what she did with her money, but Maholi refused to answer. She pleaded with her daughter that she needed that money for the house. What had she done with the money? Maholi just stared down at the floor and didn't say anything. In her mind, the money she took was rightfully hers. Maholi got Supplemental Security Income (SSI) checks from the government for her learning disability. Every time she asked her mom where that money was, she didn't answer. So Maholi felt entitled to dip into her mom's savings.

Miriam held her head in her hands and asked, "Maholi, how can you do this to me? How can you steal from me?" No matter what Miriam said, Maholi didn't respond. Desperate for an answer, she called the police, who handcuffed Maholi, and took her to the police station.

Maholi wasn't scared because she had been to a police station before. Maholi's middle school took her on a field trip to a police station and to Riker's Island in an effort to scare her out of a life of crime. It backfired; knowing what to expect at the police station made her feel more comfortable. When the police questioned her, first she told them that she didn't know anything about the money. Then she said her friend took it. Then she said that her family hit her everyday, and she needed the money to run away. They didn't believe any of it, and she spent the night at the station. They asked Miriam what she wanted to do; press or drop the charges. The only reason Miriam called the police was to get Maholi to talk. She considered pressing charges to keep her daughter out of the apartment because she was so angry. But because it was her first offense, Maholi would have gotten sent home that night anyway. Miriam decided to drop the charges because it would have cost her even more money to go through court procedures.

The next day Lisandro made a withdrawal from his bank account for $2,000 and gave it his mom. He had been saving that money for college but figured his mom needed it more than him. Miriam instructed Lisandro to stay in the apartment and make sure Maholi didn't try to run away again. In the meantime, Miriam went to a travel agent to buy plane tickets for the Dominican Republic. Lisandro suggested that Leo travel with them. He worried that Maholi might resist getting on the plane and cause a scene. If Leo went, he could handle his sister.

Over the next couple of days, Miriam scrambled to get ready for the unexpected trip. Leo got his braids done, paid his $85 ticket for hopping the subway turnstile, and said goodbye to his friends. Maholi stayed locked up in their apartment where Lisandro kept guard over her. The three left on Sunday morning at 3 a.m. to catch a 6 a.m. flight at JFK airport. Maholi didn't resist getting on the plane, but she also did not know that her mom had gotten her a one-way ticket. She was to stay indefinitely in the Dominican Republic, never to finish her studies in the United States. Leo wasn't sure how long he was going to stay, but he wasn't in a rush to get back since he wasn't in school or working.

Miriam was sad that she had to bring her daughter back to the Dominican Republic because of the poverty. She didn't see a future for her there. The family's next door neighbor worked full-time as a cook in a hospital and earned around $80 (American dollars) a month, the country's minimum wage. One of Leo's friends was so financially desperate that he contemplated selling his mom's home without telling her to get money to move to the United States.

* * *

Leo stayed for a little over a month. He wanted to return to New York because he had no money, and he missed his friends. Maholi came back 2 months later. Despite what she had done, Miriam missed her daughter.

Back in New York Maholi's family kept an even tighter grip on her than before. But it didn't stop her from skipping class. "Them classes are boring," she said. So instead of going to classes, she hung out with friends, went to hooky parties, or to the local McDonald's. Maholi made sure she was in school for her fourth period class, where attendance was taken. The school only called home if she missed that one. By her 3rd year in high school, Maholi had seven credits. She needed 30 to graduate. Everyone begged Maholi to stay in school—her mom, her boyfriend, Leo, and especially Lisandro, the father figure in the family.

10

Leo's Brother, Lisandro

The Bronx Supreme Courthouse, where Lisandro was tried

Lisandro is smart he goes to school every day . . . Lisandro wake up early and then leave to school. He always been like that, and I been asking him if he like school and he bee telling me no but that is his responsability for him know. When he graduated and he have kids his responsability are going to be his kids.

Leo's Diary, Spring 2002

Lisandro wanted a job, and his friend Charles knew someone who could help him find one. So Lisandro met him on the street one day after school. Charles, who dealt drugs, had been celebrating his birthday at a hooky and wanted Lisandro to drink with him. Lisandro didn't really want to, but he needed the job, so he drank from Charles's bottle of Alize, a cognac liquer. Two women approached Charles. Lisandro recognized one of them as a regular customer. Wanting nothing to do with the drug trade, Lisandro walked away. When the women left, Charles called him back.

Then a police car pulled up, an officer flashed his badge, and shouted, "Don't move." Lisandro assumed they had seen him drinking. The cops handcuffed them, put them in the back of the car, and drove them to booking. Lisandro thought they were going to give him a ticket and send him home since drinking underage was a violation. Instead he and Charles spent the night in a cell. There were no windows, no way of knowing what time it was. Lisandro didn't understand how people survived in jail. He felt like he was going crazy.

The next morning, Lisandro met with a public defender. The lawyer explained that Lisandro was being charged for "helping to make a sale of crack/cocaine." Lisandro was horrified. He yelped, "I didn't sell crack or cocaine. I was drinking and that's why they locked me up." The lawyer looked down at his paperwork. According to the police report, he was arrested for helping to make a narcotics sale. Since it was such a serious offense, his lawyer suggested that he plead guilty so that the court would settle on a violation as opposed to a misdemeanor or felony. But if he were to plead 'not guilty' and the case went to trial, then he would most likely go to jail if found guilty. "But I didn't sell drugs," Lisandro insisted. It didn't make sense to Lisandro to plead guilty to a crime he didn't commit. The lawyer told him that he had to return to criminal court a couple of weeks later. Because it was his first offense, he was allowed to go home.

Lisandro's mom waited for him and Charles outside the courthouse. When they got home, Lisandro ate what tasted like the best plate of *pollo frito y tostones* he had ever eaten. Jail food was terrible. Tears rolled down Miriam's face as her son begged her not to use that lawyer, who wanted him to plead guilty. Miriam had been unemployed for 2 months, and hiring a private attorney meant money that she didn't have. She scolded Lisandro for hanging out with the wrong kind of friends. Lisandro groaned. The last thing he wanted was a lecture from his mom about his friends. "I didn't sell drugs. I ain't no drug dealer."

A couple of weeks later, Lisandro, Leo, Miriam, and Charles took the subway to the criminal court house on 161st Street, off the Grand Concourse, but the judge postponed the case. The same thing happened again next time. When the case finally came before a judge, Lisandro's public defender once more encouraged him to plead guilty and accept the court's offer of a violation. Lisandro declined. He refused to plead guilty to a crime he didn't commit. The judge sent the case to trial. After a year of court appearances, the case was moved to the Bronx Supreme Court. The offer of a violation was off the table. Lisandro would be charged with a misdemeanor or possibly a felony.

Lisandro and Miriam went to see a private attorney, who had gotten a friend serving a drug sentence out of jail. The attorney was an older, balding, White man, who spoke virtually no Spanish. After reviewing Lisandro's case, he concluded that he had a good chance of winning because it was Lisandro's first offense. But before he would take the case, he needed $3,000. Miriam didn't understand, and when Lisandro translated, she protested, "$3,000! I don't have $3,000." The lawyer added that he normally charged more for a case like Lisandro's, but since he seemed like a "good kid" and his family didn't have a lot of money, he lowered the price.

Three thousand dollars seemed like an impossible amount of money, but Miriam couldn't bear the thought of her son being convicted of drug charges. So she dipped into her rent money, paid some other bills late, and begged her friends and family to lend her money. She managed to scrounge up the $3,000.

On the day of the trial, Lisandro and Miriam waited in line at the Courthouse for 20 minutes before going through the metal detector. They sat on a bench in the back of the courtroom. A few minutes later, Lisandro's lawyer arrived, looked at them as if he had never seen them before, and walked to the front of the courtroom. He placed his coat on one of the vacant wooden benches and left the room, nodding to Lisandro. Lisandro and his mom got up and followed him out. The lawyer told Lisandro that he needed $2,000 more to continue working on his case. The case had taken longer than he had anticipated, and the $3,000 only covered pretrial work. The lawyer walked back into the courtroom, leaving Lisandro to translate for his mom. "$2,000!" But he said we only had to pay him $3,000. I don't have $2,000," Miriam said in a panicked voice. She was already in debt from the previous $3,000. Lisandro didn't respond, and they returned to the courtroom, Miriam on the verge of tears.

Lisandro scanned the courtroom. All of the people who worked there were White. The judge was an old White man. Lisandro's lawyer was an old White man. The woman typing on the "court machine" was White. Even the Spanish interpreter was White. Lisandro turned to the defendants' benches. There were four Black people and three Hispanics waiting for their trials. As they waited for the court proceedings to begin, Lisandro's lawyer spoke casually with the other court employees about his weekend and sports. He acted as if it were just another day.

The judge called Lisandro's name. He walked over to his lawyer, a court-appointed interpreter at his side. The judge asked the prosecutor about his witness. He said the witness was testifying in another case, but should be there soon. After a few minutes of waiting, the judge postponed the case. "We got lucky," the lawyer said to Lisandro. "This will give your family more time to come up with the $2,000." Miriam asked if they could pay in installments. Lisandro translated, which irritated the lawyer. He wanted the money in one payment. Miriam started to ask Lisandro to "Explain to him that we don't have that kind of money." Before she could finish, the lawyer brusquely told them that coming up with the money was not his problem. He walked away before they could say another word.

Miriam and Lisandro returned to the same courtroom 2 months later. When Lisandro's lawyer arrived and asked if he had $2,000, Lisandro said, "No." He reminded Lisandro that if he didn't receive more money, he could no longer work on the case. The lawyer walked away and read the newspaper.

When the judge called Lisandro's name, he joined the lawyer. The judge said that he wanted to make sure the defendant understood his options regarding his case and their consequences. If Lisandro were to plead not guilty, but was later found guilty by a jury, he most likely would have to serve time in jail. If, however, the defendant decided to plead guilty, then he would be offered a plea bargain by the courts, and would be charged with "youth status offender." He would be given 5 years of probation. The judge said he didn't want the defendant to plead guilty if he was not guilty, but he also reminded him that he had no control over how the jury would decide the case.

Lisandro whispered to his lawyer, who in turn told the court. "Your honor, the defendant would like to know if he could have a few minutes with his family." "That's fine," the judged responded. Lisandro, his mother, and lawyer stepped outside the courtroom, where the lawyer explained that Charles had had his trial and pleaded guilty. Lisandro was now being charged "in concert" with Charles because Charles had told the courts that they had worked together on the drug transaction. If Lisandro were to go through a jury trial, not only would it be his word against the undercover policewoman, who said that Lisandro had directly spoken to her, but against Charles's testimony as well.

Several minutes later, they returned to the courtroom, and the attorney told the judge, "Your honor, my client would like to change his plea from not guilty to guilty." The judge said that he was going to ask Lisandro a series of questions, and if at any moment he didn't understand them, the judge would stop and have Lisandro's lawyer explain what he had just said. The questions began, "Are you pleading guilty to the crime to which you have been charged?" "Yes," Lisandro answered. "Have you been coerced into changing your plea from not guilty to guilty by your lawyer or anyone else? Lisandro said "No." The judge asked if his plea of guilty was the truth, and Lisandro hesitated before saying, "Yes." The judge asked him to describe the crime he had committed. "You mean what actually happened?" responded Lisandro. His lawyer whispered to him, and Lisandro said, "I helped sell drugs." Miriam didn't understand English, but she knew her son had just told the courtroom that he had sold drugs. She moaned and doubled over as if punched in the stomach. The judge asked Lisandro if he pleaded guilty to the charge of selling crack/cocaine as charged. Lisandro said, "Yes." With that, Lisandro's mom walked out of the courtroom crying.

In the end, Lisandro had accepted a plea bargain of "Youth Status Offender," the equivalent to a felony conviction for underage offenders. There would be no jail time, but he would be on probation for the next 5 years. He would have to see a parole officer once a month. Lisandro could not leave the state without first getting permission from his parole officer, and he would not be able to leave the country until after he served his 5 years of probation. If he got arrested again, he would likely be sent to jail and possibly deported.

*   *   *

Lisandro did his best to stay out of trouble. All he wanted was to graduate from high school and get out of the Bronx. If he passed all of his classes and Regents exams, he could graduate by the end of the year. While Lisandro went to most of his classes, he almost never did homework. He rationalized, "You spend 8 hours in school and you gotta relax because you tired." Instead Lisandro spent his afternoons working at a Manhattan grocery for $6.00 an hour stocking shelves, helping customers, sweeping the floors, and taking out the trash. He spent most of the money he earned on new clothes and his girlfriend, Betty. He also gave some to his mom to help with rent and the other household expenses. On his afternoons off, Lisandro participated in the YMCA's after-school program. The basketball games and the field trips were his favorites.

He spent the rest of his free time with Betty. Born and raised in Harlem, Betty was Dominican with bright pretty eyes, straight black hair, caramel skin, and an aggressive confidence. She was smart and never without an opinion. He picked her up and walked her home almost every night from her grocery job in Harlem. They talked on the phone when they weren't together, and he bought her a promise ring one year for Christmas. Betty finished high school a semester early and was planning on attending Johnson and Wales College in Providence, Rhode Island, where her family had just bought a house. Lisandro was happy for Betty, but it bothered him that she was always one step ahead of him.

By spring semester, Lisandro was almost sure that he was going to graduate, so he went to his high school counselor to ask about college. The only two people Lisandro knew who were either in college or going to go to college were Betty and a neighborhood friend. He had heard about Johnson and Wales College from Betty, and his friend had told him about the Higher Education Opportunity Program (HEOP), a state-sponsored program for low-income students who didn't do well in high school, but showed potential to do well in college. Students had to attend an intensive remedial summer program. If they maintained a 2.0 GPA, the program subsidized their tuition at participating higher education institutions within New York State. Lisandro's high school counselor helped him fill out an application to Johnson and Wales College, the City University of New York (CUNY), a FAFSA form (Free Application for Federal Student Aid), and an application for the HEOP.

*   *   *

Several months later, Lisandro received a letter of admission to Johnson and Wales College. He accepted the offer, filled out a housing form and completed the necessary financial aid documents. Based on his family income, Lisandro had received the maximum government student loan of $17,000. He got permission from his parole officer to study out of state and, as far as Lisandro knew, he was set for college in the fall. He couldn't wait.

Then the bill came from Johnson and Wales College. He had 2 weeks to pay the outstanding $8,000 for room and board. He couldn't afford it, so he couldn't attend. His school counselor suggested going to a community college for a year, earning some money, and then transferring to Johnson and Wales. He went to register at Bronx Community College, but was too late. He was told to come back the following month to register for spring semester. But spring term came and went, and Lisandro didn't register for school. His plan was to begin that summer. But when he started having problems at home, Lisandro decided to move out first and then go to school. He went back to his high school job.

The next summer he participated in the New York State's Higher Education Opportunity Program intensive summer program for promising disadvantaged students in preparation for his enrollment at an aeronautical college in Queens, New York. When school began, he studied during the day and worked at night.

After Betty graduated with an associate's degree in accounting, they began living together in an apartment in Harlem. Betty looked for an accounting job and planned to attend a 4-year college in the city. But everything changed when she found out that she was pregnant.

Lisandro quit school and got a second job to save money for a proper baby shower. He wanted Betty's family to see that he was prepared to be a father. So he worked one job from 9 to 5 and his second one from 6 to 10. On his days off, he prepared for the shower. Betty kept her bank job right up until a few weeks before giving birth.

Lisbeth was born on May 4, 2005. She had big brown eyes, Betty's complexion, and black curls.

11

Leo's Friend, Aneudys

Aneudys, after serving time in upstate New York

My goal for the future is to not get arrested. I know it sound stupid but my friend got out of jail. He was 4 days in there and he said that I wish that none of us be there. . . . My goal of not getting arrested I going to accomplish by staind away from my friend that always be getting into trouble. Trouble is not for me but since I live around here I had to be friendly and if they act stupid you have to do something about it. When I said act stupid is like trying to fight you for little things like because you blood and I am a Latin King we had to fight. And if you not you will have a knew nick name "Pussy" everybody will call you "Pussy." That the things that some of my friends get in trouble for

Leo's Diary, Spring 2002

IT TOOK A MOMENT for Leo to realize he was barefoot in the middle of winter. It happened so fast. One minute he was walking back from his friend's apartment, and the next minute a group of guys were stealing his coat and shoes. Leo picked himself off the ground, his feet burning from the cold and snow, and walked to the nearest police station, where an officer took his statement and said they would investigate.

Leo was angry. That coat cost him $250, his shoes cost $100, and he had $50 in his pocket. He called Juan Carlos, Carlos, and a few others, including his friend Aneudys. Although small in stature, Aneudys was never shy about throwing a punch. They went looking for the muggers but didn't find them.

A few days later, Leo and Aneudys found a kid wearing a coat just like Leo's, so they jumped him. At first Leo felt bad, because he wasn't certain that it was the same kid who stole his coat. But when the kid yelled, "Fuck Dominicans," he didn't feel so bad anymore. They sold the coat for $130. Aneudys got $50 and Leo kept $80. He gave $30 to his mom to pay bills, though she never knew its source, and used the rest to buy two new shirts.

Aneudys graduated from high school and got a job as a security guard. One night after work, Aneudys and a group of friends were on the subway heading downtown to a party when one of his friends spotted a guy who looked like a Blood. He asked him, "You Blood?" The guy said, "No," but Aneudys's friend punched him anyway. Aneudys hit him in the head with his umbrella while another friend stabbed him. Passengers fled to other cars.

One of them reported the fight to a subway conductor. Aneudys and his friends tried to move to another car, but the door wouldn't open, so Aneudys sat down and tried to blend in with the other passengers. The man who reported the crime, walked through the train with a police officer and pointed to Aneudys. They handcuffed him and took him to the station with two of his friends. Aneudys wasn't afraid because he had been arrested before. During his junior year in high school, he and his friends jumped a guy who was bullying another kid. The police caught them, but Aneudys didn't take it seriously because everyone was cracking jokes in the jail cell. In the end, the charges were dropped.

This time, the charges were 2nd and 3rd degree assault, rioting, and gang assault. He could potentially get 5 to 15 years in prison. A public defender was appointed and Aneudys pleaded not guilty. His court appearances became one canceled trial date after another. He waited 9 months for his trial.

While waiting, Aneudys got into a fight over a girl. He was stabbed many times and went into a coma. Only family members were permitted to visit. Leo called Aneudys's mom everyday and asked, "¿Como está hoy?" She wept and told him that he still hadn't opened his eyes. Leo thought his friend was going to die. Although he had lost several good friends over the years, this would be the most painful loss. Four days later, Aneudys regained consciousness. Leo visited him as soon as he was permitted. His friend looked awful. He didn't know what to say, so he asked, "You in pain?" Aneudys was released in a few days with over 100 staples.

Several months later, Aneudys sat next to his court-appointed lawyer in a New York City court. He was sentenced to between 16 months to 4 years at Washington Correctional Facility in Upstate New York for the stabbing his friend committed. The night before Aneudys went to jail, he stayed up all night drinking with Leo and some of his DDP (Dominicans Don't Play) friends. When it was time to go, Leo promised, "I'm gonna come visit you."

* * *

Eight months later, Leo and Juan Carlos stood under an awning in the rain at 2 in the morning outside Yankee Stadium. About 25 other people waited with them for minivans, which charged $35 for a round trip ticket, to take them to the prison. All but one of the other passengers, a Black man, were women of color. During the 4½-hour trip, Juan Carlos slept, and Leo watched the movie *Traffic*, the antidrug Academy Award-winning film, playing on the bus.

When they arrived, Leo and Juan Carlos filled out the required guest paperwork, left their personal belongings in the visitor lockers, and were denied permission to bring into the prison the cleats that Aneudys's mom sent for her son.

When their numbers were called, they entered the visitor center for Aneudys's cell block. The sound of iron doors shutting made Juan Carlos uncomfortable. "I don't like the feeling of being locked in." It didn't bother Leo so much.

After going through three more sets of doors, they were seated at a table assigned to Aneudys and his visitors. It was 8 a.m. Near them, Juan Carlos saw a little Black girl who hopped back and forth between an inmate and her mother. "Damn," he said, "If I ever have a kid, I ain't getting locked up." At 8:30, Aneudys arrived and smiled broadly. They told him the latest gossip from the block while Aneudys described what it was like to be in prison. He said it wasn't so bad, almost like a "ghetto vacation."

The one thing Aneudys didn't like were the corrections officers. He told of being in a shower when a fight broke out. A guard asked Aneudys, whose chest was red from the shower's hot water, who hit him. When he said he had not been hit, the guard slapped him. He continued denying that he had been assaulted, and the officer continued hitting him. Finally, the guard threatened to put him in "the box," solitary confinement. In the end, for lack of proof, Aneudys was permitted to remain in his cell.

At exactly 2 p.m., visiting time was over. Lovers kissed goodbye, moms tearfully hugged their sons, kids cried as they said goodbye to Dad. Juan Carlos and Leo gave Aneudys a half hug and promised to return again. They watched Aneudys walk back to his cell with his head down and his feet dragging. Juan commented, "He says he's doing all right, but I know it is harder than he says."

Juan Carlos promised himself that he would try to visit Aneudys again in December, particularly because none of his other friends had visited. Leo decided this would be the last time he'd visit Aneudys. The 10-hour journey was too long and too expensive. Plus he wanted to use his time and energy to find a job and finish school. He bought some dressy shoes for job interviews and looked into another GED program.

12

No Way Out

Leo's grave (top right) at the family mausoleum in the Domincan Republic

Today is Sunday and I found out that someone got kill. . . . His name was Jorge and he use to live in Valinetine Ave and 187. Around 5:00 my friend gave me this news and I coulding belive it . . . today was Jorge funeral. After I saw him I coulding stop putting his picture of him in that toonstone in my head. When we got there everybody was quit his mom was criying. This is my first funeral. I felt different there that Smell and to see Jorge in that toonstone it was scary. Seen that young face . . . there it was scary. . . . When I came home I coulding eat nothing, I was kind of sick.

Leo's Diary, Spring 2002

I knew that when I came to be 15 year old something bad was going
to happen. . . . Maybe one of these day I will get killed or something or
maybe get stab. . . . Every time a go somewhere out of the neighborhood
I be walking scare. I dont even feel safe around [here].

Leo's diary, Spring 2002

O N SUNDAY, OCTOBER 30, 2005, Leo was shot and killed by a
police officer on Creston Avenue. There were as many stories
about what happened as there were people watching the fight
that led to the shooting. Leo was a bystander. Leo was trying to break
up the fight. Leo was one of the fighters. He had a knife. He didn't have
a knife. There were two police officers, and one fired at Leo because he
threatened them or he lunged at them with a knife. Or they panicked
in the face of the sizeable Halloween crowd. Leo didn't hear them, they
didn't hear him, or they made a mistake, taking Leo's effort to surren-
der the knife or show that he didn't have a weapon for an attack.

This much is certain. Two shots were fired by a police sergeant. The
first gunshot missed Leo, but the second hit Leo in the side. The police
closed off the street and handcuffed Leo on the ground with his hands
behind his back. He lay face down in a pool of blood.

Word got around fast about what happened. His friend Juan Carlos
found out by phone. He was in his dorm room at Mount Saint Mary College in Newburgh, New York, when he listened to his messages from
Lisandro, Maholi, and a few others but couldn't grasp what they said.
He called Lisandro who told him, *"Ven a la ciudad que fue la policía
que lo mató a Leo."* ("Come to the city. The police killed Leo").

Not sure what to do, Juan Carlos went looking for his and Leo's friend
Carlos, who lived in a neighboring dorm. In between sobs, he managed
to get the words out, "The police killed Leo," Carlos quietly put on his
"hoody" and said, "Let's go to the city." Juan Carlos blamed himself.
Why hadn't he convinced Leo to spend the weekend with him and Carlos at college instead of going to that Halloween party in the Bronx?

Ana and Leo had not spoken in 3 months, but Ana called Betty
that night to check up on Leo. Betty could tell by Ana's voice that she
hadn't heard the news. After a long pause, she told Ana, "Leo passed
away." Ana left her restaurant job hyperventilating, and went directly
to Leo's apartment.

*   *   *

That night, Leo's family and friends gathered on the street for a vigil.
Lisandro stared at the dried blood on the sidewalk and wiped the tears

from his eyes. Girls hugged each other. Others prayed. Juan Carlos and Carlos looked at the basketball hoop that hung above the bloody sidewalk. It was ironic that Leo had been shot there, his favorite spot to shoot a "three-pointer." When Leo talked about the block, that spot was it, the place they had spent countless hours playing basketball and splashing around in *la pompa* during the summer.

People who didn't know Leo came for the drama. Leo was the latest news in the neighborhood. A friend couldn't stand the gawkers staring at the bloody sidewalk, so he poured wax over it. Others helped until only wax could be seen on the sidewalk. At Miriam's, a friend read from the Bible while Ana and others looked at pictures of Leo. Miriam sat on the couch and stared at the wall.

The next night a mural was painted on the street where Leo was shot. It was the expected way to memorialize someone from the neighborhood. A graffiti artist painted a picture of Leo taken from a cell phone camera. The mural was large—10 feet high and 12 feet wide. At the center was a picture of Leo in his red baseball cap with a gold chain around his neck. Leo's big brown eyes stared at passerby's. On the bottom right hand corner, the names of Leo's family members were written in big silver letters. On the opposite corner, the names of about 50 of Leo's closest friends were written in yellow paint. Most graffitied walls in the neighborhood eventually got sprayed over by other taggers, but not this one. It was an extraordinary mural that no one dared disrespect.

* * *

The police never contacted Miriam. When she went to the police station, they refused to tell her why they shot Leo. They couldn't release his possessions either—his wallet, house keys and the $1000 gold chain that Leo had borrowed from Carlos. All of it was evidence.

Miriam didn't trust the police and was terrified that they were going to break into her apartment, afraid they had bugged her phones. But her worst fear was that they would hurt another one of her kids. Miriam refused to let Maholi walk to school alone.

On Tuesday, Juan Carlos, Lisandro, and Carlos went to Jacobi Hospital to identify Leo's body. Juan Carlos looked through the glass window in the hospital basement and saw his best friend's body. It was so much more terrible to see him there than just knowing he was dead. Carlos waited outside. He was too afraid to look. Lisandro stood immobile in front of the window, unable to speak, unable to cry.

Miriam didn't know how she was going to pay for her son's burial.

She had used all of her money to help her brother with recent legal problems. In the end, donations from friends and family paid for most of the expenses. After comparing funeral prices and services, they decided to go with Ortiz funeral home.

Leo had been there before for the funerals of his friends Jorge, Naldo, and Doble. Jorge had been stabbed. Naldo was a drug dealer, who had gotten shot twice in the back of the head. Doble was killed in a fight over a girl.

For a little over $2,000, Ortiz funeral home would pick up Leo's body from the hospital, provide a basic casket, host a 6-hour wake with artificial flowers, and send the body to the Dominican Republic. It was $3,000 cheaper to bury Leo in the Dominican Republic than New York. Plus, he could be buried next to his grandmother Teresa, who had died exactly 1 month earlier. Miriam scrounged up money for plane tickets. Lisandro requested permission from his parole officer to leave the country, but his request was denied.

* * *

Lisandro, Miriam, and Juan Carlos went to the funeral home to sort out the details of the wake. Lisandro carried the outfit he had picked out for Leo. The only thing missing was the socks. They worried about what color to get and chose white.

When they arrived at the funeral home, the director explained all of the things that could go wrong in delivering the body to the Dominican Republic. They would do their best but couldn't guarantee that the coffin would arrive on the designated day because of extenuating factors, like customs approval.

The next order of business was the death certificate. The director asked standard questions, like Leo's full name, address, and occupation. When he asked his father's name, Miriam was so flustered she couldn't remember. Lisandro answered, "Andre."

When the death certificate was complete, the director asked, "How do you want his hair and facial hair done?" Miriam gazed back blankly. Lisandro pointed to himself and said, "Like mine, a small goatee. Can you cut some of his braids for me?" The director said, "Okay."

The final topic was payment. They had up until the day of the wake.

* * *

Miriam, Maholi, and Lisandro were the first to arrive at the wake on Friday afternoon. Leo laid in a white casket with his hands folded across his stomach, his black and gold beads wrapped around his hands. It looked like a wax version of Leo with a gray skin tone. The mascara that Miriam had carefully applied to her eyes streamed down her face. Lisandro pried her away from the coffin and walked her to a small sofa about 10 feet away where she wailed, sucking in gasps of air for almost the entire 6-hour wake.

By 5 p.m., the funeral room was packed. Girls walked up to the casket and burst into tears. They held Leo's hand. They kissed his forehead. At times the room was silent, except for Leo's mom. Her crying was constant. Lisandro greeted people in a half daze. Maholi sometimes comforted friends during bouts of crying; other times friends comforted her.

Juan Carlos arrived at 5:30. He thought he had cried all he could, but when he saw Leo lying in a casket, he walked out of the funeral home and collapsed on the sidewalk.

About an hour later, Carlos arrived with the same outfit as Juan Carlos's—a t-shirt with a picture of Leo scanned from a cell phone photo, a black sports coat and baggy jeans. Making t-shirts for a wake was the custom on the block, and Leo's closest friends had carefully designed theirs with the words "RIP Leo" on the front. Tears rolled down Carlos's face. People offered words of support, but he couldn't speak.

There were so many people in attendance that they spilled out into the hallway. After a group prayer, the minister invited people to speak. In typical Juan Carlos fashion, he went first and told the packed room what it felt like to lose his brother. Leo's mom stood up and thanked everyone for coming. She started to say something but broke down midsentence and crumbled into the couch. Lisandro declared that he wasn't going to say goodbye to his brother because Leo had been too full of life to be gone now. Maholi talked about her relationship with Leo and how much she was going to miss their fighting.

The wake ended abruptly at 8 p.m. when the funeral home staff carried the casket away to begin preparations for the 6 a.m. flight. Miriam and Maholi went back to their apartment and tried to sleep. Juan Carlos, Carlos, and Lisandro went to a party in Leo's building, where they drank to dull the pain. A group of people, including Juan Carlos, ended up in front of Leo's mural. When an argument almost turned into a fight, Juan Carlos got in the middle and tried to break it up. He didn't notice the cop until he pushed Juan Carlos and told him, "Get off my block." Between the loss he felt and the alcohol, Juan Carlos couldn't hold his temper. He pushed the cop back and yelled, "What are you going to do, kill me too?" He pulled his arm back to punch the cop, but a friend grabbed him away. Juan Carlos decided to go home for the night.

At 2 a.m., Lisandro returned to his apartment with Carlos and four other friends. Everyone was drunk except Lisandro. Miriam screamed at him for coming home so late. Miriam, her boyfriend, Maholi, Ana, Leo's half-sister, and a cousin left for the airport immediately.

*   *   *

When they landed in the Dominican Republic, an ambulance carried Leo's coffin from the airport to his grandma's house. At least 100 family members and friends attended. There was crying, even howling. When uncles and cousins opened the casket in the living room, the crowd rushed in. Some touched Leo. Many kissed his forehead. He was paler and Miriam couldn't understand why his lips had turned a disturbing shade of grayish white. It looked even less like Leo than at the wake in New York. Every half hour they closed the casket to protect the body against the heat. Miriam slept that night for the first time since Leo had been shot on the floor next to the casket.

Ana and Maholi slept in Miriam's new home, a block away. Completed just 4 months before, it had a garage, living room, spacious kitchen, and three bedrooms replete with tiled floors, light fixtures, ceiling fans, and sliding glass doors to the patio. Miriam had borrowed money from her brother, who worked in a Boston hotel, to replace the funds Maholi had taken.

When Maholi saw her father, she ignored him. She was mad at Moreno for blaming her mom for Leo's death. After all, she thought, where had he been the last 19 years of Leo's life?

When Miriam and Moreno had spoken on the phone earlier that week, Moreno reminded her that he never wanted his kids in the United States. That was her idea. It was also her fault, he thought, because she had worked at night when she should have been home with the kids. He used to think Miriam was "alright," but not anymore. Not after Leo died.

Maholi changed her attitude toward her dad when he offered to take her, Ana, and her step-sister for a ride around town. Ana giggled uncontrollably at Moreno's stories, and the three girls happily ate the food and drank the beer he bought them. He also let them drink rum, something Leo's mom never would have allowed during the traditional Dominican 9 days of mourning.

One minute Ana cried because she missed Leo so much, and the next, because she couldn't forgive him. People talked about the hooky parties and other girls. Ana saw girls crying too hard at his wake to have just been friends, and she almost hit that girl who had kissed him on the lips. But when Leo's father joked, "Put a skirt on a broom handle and Leo would have fucked her," Ana told him that was disrespectful; he apologized and said she was the only one Leo really loved.

* * *

The next day began with a mass at the house followed by a procession down the street led by a drummer and trumpeter. The casket was loaded onto a pick-up truck; family and friends followed behind. Cousin Ruddy ran along the procession, videotaping as much as he could because Lisandro couldn't be there.

They arrived at the same burial site where Leo and his family had gathered a month earlier to bury Leo's grandmother. Uncle Radhame and Uncle Nelson opened the casket. Miriam bent down inches from her son's face and cried. Neighbors wailed in the background. Ruddy hugged his sister and sobbed desperately, "He's gone. He's gone. He's never coming to visit us again." After a few minutes, someone pulled Miriam away from Leo. The casket was shut and locked. Ruddy took a hammer and smashed its lid so that thieves would not steal it. He pounded it over and over until his uncle said, "Ya. Basta!" When they lifted the casket to put it next to his grandma's casket, the casket didn't fit. So they smashed it until it slid into its designated space. Uncle Nelson covered the opening with cement. The burial was over and so began the traditional Dominican 9 days of mourning.

Each day, the family held a mass in Leo's grandma's house at 6 p.m. After the prayers, the family served food to visitors, usually a soup or a pureed salami and cheese mix on white bread. During the period of mourning, family and friends were not supposed to drink, listen to music, dance, or indulge in anything pleasurable. It was considered a form of respect toward the dead.

But Moreno wanted Ana, Maholi, and his other daughter to have fun in the DR. He took them to his home, stopping to pick up two big bottles of beer and four plastic cups. He told them, "Leo was my friend. I've lost everything now. I want to have another son to replace Leo." Ana looked at Moreno in disbelief and told him that he couldn't replace Leo. "*Leo era único.*" He said, "Leo was the only one who cared about me. Maholi never calls me. Neither does Lisandro. Leo was the only one." They drove back to Miriam's house when they finished their beer.

* * *

At the conclusion of the mourning period, Miriam, Maholi, and Ana flew back to New York. Miriam tried to resume her life, but there were too many memories of Leo in the apartment. She wanted to move out of the city.

The problem was lack of money, which only got worse when she was fired in December. Due to a transit strike, she had been unable to get to work. So she spent her days looking for another job, going to church, and taking care of the puppy she had brought back from the Dominican Republic. Maholi coped by convincing herself that Leo wasn't dead, but just visiting the Dominican Republic. Ana ended up living at Lisandro's and Betty's apartment when her brother kicked her out for going to the DR rather than helping their parents. She also lost her job because she had been absent from work while in the Dominican Republic. Lisandro eased his pain by drinking, which he rationalized by "drinking in Leo's name." Juan Carlos and Carlos went back to school the Monday after the wake. Carlos was happy to get away from the Bronx and all of its reminders of Leo. Juan Carlos, on the other hand, wasn't sure how he was going to get through the semester. He felt depressed. He spoke to the school's priest. He wrote in a journal and made a Web site for Leo.

* * *

Miriam wanted Leo's things back from the police. But she had to wait 6 months until the investigation was complete. Then she was told that she needed a letter from the district attorney. After receiving it 2 months following her request, Miriam went to the police property retrieval office and gave it to an officer seated behind a gate. She told Miriam she would need a voucher from the officer who arrested Leo. Realizing how difficult it would be for her to talk with the man who killed her son, the officer offered to call the police station so they could fax the forms. But she told Miriam she would still need to obtain the paperwork granting permission to release Leo's belongings. The man required to sign that form—a big guy with tattoos covering his arms—refused to do so until he got a written statement verifying that the police investigation had been completed.

Miriam waited in a hot, windowless office for the fax to arrive. An hour later, a disgruntled officer opened the gate and barked at Miriam to sign several more forms. Miriam then gave all of the documents to another officer behind the gated window of property retrieval, where she had begun her day 5 hours earlier. He told her Leo's possessions still could not be released because one of the letters was a photocopy, not an original. Luckily, the first officer Miriam had spoken with overheard the conversation and intervened.

On some pages of the voucher, there was an orange sticker with the word, "Biotoxins." The officer explained that some of the items had blood on them. Miriam started crying. The officer shuffled through the paperwork a little faster and brought her Leo's belongings in plastic bags. Miriam carefully checked each item to make sure everything listed on the voucher was in the bags. The white doo-rag that he wore was stained in blood as were his wallet, keys, and a notepad with girls' numbers. Things were missing, important things that Miriam wanted back like Leo's shoes, jeans, underpants, and socks.

Miriam had to go to another office on Long Island City to get them. When she called for directions, the officer said the office was accessible only by car, which required that she wait until Lisandro had a day off so he could drive her there.

When Miriam got home, she and her brother Siso examined each item in Leo's wallet carefully—an old paycheck stub, a money transfer Juan Carlos had sent when Leo was in the DR, old receipts. Maybe she thought the items would make her feel closer to Leo—perhaps offer some insight into what happened that night. But the contents were too painful to keep, so she threw most of them away.

*   *   *

Two weeks later, Lisandro, Juan Carlos, and Miriam went to pick up the remainder of Leo's possessions in a warehouse in an industrial park, surrounded by dilapidated and abandoned buildings. Miriam gave the paperwork to the officer on duty, who warned her that it might take awhile because the items were stored in another warehouse a few minutes away. So the three got coffee and waited. About 1½ hours later, Miriam asked a different officer for help. At first he couldn't find her paperwork, but finally located them under other paperwork and mumbled that the first officer probably never did anything with them.

He drew a map on a napkin, directing them to the site where they could pick up the remaining possessions. They couldn't find the building, which turned out to be a structure that appeared abandoned. Once they found it, they couldn't figure out how to get in. Having no luck finding an entrance at the front of the building, they went around the side where the door seemed to be sealed. Lisandro banged on it until two police officers opened the door.

With arms crossed, the officers asked what they wanted. It seemed like a strange question because the officer from the other building had just called. Miriam handed them the paperwork. Without looking at the papers, one officer said they couldn't get the items without a letter from the district attorney. Juan Carlos pointed out the district attorney's letter. The officer then said he couldn't give them anything without a letter from the detective who conducted the investigation. They showed him that letter too. He told them to wait and left with their sheaf of papers. The possibility that the officer and the paperwork would never return seemed all too real.

The officer reappeared with more forms to sign and then produced three large, sealed envelopes. Miriam insisted on checking to make sure that all the vouchered items were in the envelopes. When she opened them, the smell of dried blood filled the room. Lisandro pulled out a balled-up pair of jeans, stained deep purple, bloody underpants and t-shirt, and Carlos's chain.

They went home.

PART III

WHAT CHANGED?

13

The Old Neighborhood Meets the New

Arthur, Debby, Barry, and Jim at Arthur's apartment during their first reunion

Take away the music; take away the graffiti; take away the gates . . . take away the drugs and shootings and all that stuff [and] instead of me, Leo, and Carlos on the corner, it's Jim and his friends . . . playing football.

Juan Carlos

No.

Debby and Jim
Winter, 2002

A FEW YEARS BEFORE LEO DIED, Arthur and Laura brought together past and present residents of the Bronx neighborhood to compare the worlds in which they grew up. Arthur invited three of his childhood friends—Barry Bernstein, Debby Fleischner, and Jim Welbur—to meet with Leo, Juan Carlos, Carlos, and Lisandro. Over 2 weekends, they talked about their experiences on Creston Avenue, the similarities and the differences.

Barry Bernstein, a year ahead of Arthur in school, was his best friend as a boy. They lived in the same apartment building. His parents, like Arthur's, were born in this country. His mother graduated from high school, and his father didn't. His older brother and sister went to college. Barry attended Pace University; married right after college; had one son; now lives in New Jersey with his wife, a retired teacher; and spent his career as a teacher in the Bronx. At the time Barry met the boys, he was 54, with a salt and pepper beard.

Debby Fleischner lived in the same building and was a grade behind Arthur. She was a nurse in upstate New York. A graduate of the University of California, Berkeley, she followed her siblings—lawyers and a doctor—to a top university. Debby's parents, who came from Eastern Europe, had little if any formal education and were most comfortable speaking Yiddish. Her dad was an upholsterer, and her mother worked at home as a seamstress, later in a factory. At the time she met the boys, Debby, a mother of two and the wife of a union official, was 53 years old, thin, and attractive, with graying dark straight hair.

Jim Welber lived in the building next door to Arthur's. They must have played a million games of punch ball, stickball, and scully together. He graduated from City College of New York, became a teacher, and advanced to a middle school principalship in the Bronx and then the New York suburbs. Jim, a first born, aged 54, had graying, stylishly cut hair and glasses. He remained handsome, but had gained a little weight. The plan was to lose the additional pounds when he and his wife, a teacher, retired to Florida in a few months. Jim had a daughter from his first marriage. His parents, like Debby's, came from Eastern Europe and had little or no formal education. Yiddish was also their preferred language. His dad worked at various times as a trucker, butcher, barber, and newspaper and candy seller. His mother had jobs as a seamstress and a cashier. Jim was the wildest of the four. He had cut classes, played hooky, ignored homework, and had sex in high school.

The two generations first met in the summer in 2002, right before Leo started high school. Carlos lived in Arthur's old apartment, Leo and Lisandro lived two blocks up the street, and Juan Carlos lived two blocks over. Both Juan Carlos and Carlos had finished their 2nd year of high school and were doing poorly academically. Neither was sure he would graduate. In contrast, Lisandro was a high school senior, who hoped to attend college, but had no idea what he needed to do to get there.

* * *

The boys and Arthur's friends talked for hours. Their conversations were not so much about the great issues in urban America—poverty, race, and violence—but about how two groups of teenagers lived their lives on the same piece of real estate 4 decades apart. Arthur and his friends took the boys to the places that were important to them when they grew up, and the boys showed them the world in which they lived. Arthur and his friends showed the boys where they played ball and where they broke windows. The boys showed them their favorite basketball court, the spots where people were killed, and the corners where drug dealers plied their trade.

Arthur and his friends spent a day asking the boys questions, and they, in turn, spent the next day asking Arthur and his friends questions. Some of the conversations took place in Arthur's old bedroom; some in a local school; some on the streets and the sites that were important in their lives; and some took place at Arthur's home, the president's house at Teachers College. Arthur and his friends showed the boys how they played punch ball on the street under Carlos's window. It was a spirited demonstration, but a truly pathetic performance. In turn, the boys invited them to play basketball. Jim accepted and the rest watched. Jim had terrible back pain for days afterward. They ate the foods each group grew up with. In truth, a few looked at unfamiliar cuisine and passed.

They discussed almost everything that is part of a teenager's life— from friends, family, and school—to sex, partying, and fights. The boys asked how often Arthur's friends had fights. Rarely, they said. The most recent any of them could remember was junior high school. The boys said fighting, having "beef," was a way of life for them. They got into fights because someone wanted their coat or because they were in the wrong gang or no gang or because their skin was the wrong color, or because they were in the wrong place at the wrong time, or because someone looked at them the wrong way or put down a girlfriend, or for a host of other reasons. They described a world of continual fighting, which might involve fists, feet, knives, guns, bottles, or anything else that could be used as a weapon, punctuated by periods of hunting for people to fight and being hunted by others who wanted to fight with them. For Leo and his friends the threat never disappeared. Leo explained that more and more places that once seemed safe to him weren't anymore—not the block where he lived, not the school he attended. The boys said they had to fight if they wanted respect. They had to join a gang if they wanted protection on the street or even in school. They painted a Darwinian picture of life on the block.

In contrast, when Arthur grew up there were no gangs, except the mythologized Fordham Baldies with whom he had no contact. Jim said he had run into a gang. When Arthur and his friends had fights, it was with their hands and occasionally feet. They could count the number of fights they had on the fingers of two hands.

The boys wanted to know whether Arthur's friends had hookies. The term was unfamiliar to them. The boys defined it. Jim had been to such events. Barry and Debby were amazed as much by Jim as the idea of cutting school to dance, drink, and have sex. Barry and Arthur were terrible dancers and like Debby hadn't had sex while they lived on the block. This was the boys' chance to be shocked; they wondered whether sexual abstinence was unhealthy given the high stress in young people's lives.

* * *

The greatest disparity in attitudes between the generations was over school. The oldsters described school as a job; you were supposed to be there every day. You had to do all of your homework every night. Their futures depended upon it.

Current residents were surprised. School was boring. They did homework irregularly, if at all. Spending 8 hours a day in school was enough. Requiring homework on top of that was unreasonable. In fact, going to school every day was unnecessary. They debated over how many classes and school days one could or should miss. Lisandro was offered as a model of success. He did not do homework, cut classes sometimes, and periodically attended hookies; yet he had an 84% average.

Once again, Jim was the bridge between generations. He did what the boys did, but he argued for moderation. Jim would cut classes and ignore assignments only as long as he was not in danger of failing. He made sure he was in class for tests, which was not the case for several of the boys.

The conversation turned to report cards. What was a good grade? For all of Arthur's friends, grades under 85% were problematic. For the boys, a passing grade of 65% was good. Debby told a story, like

Arthur's, of bringing home a grade high in the 90s and having her father ask what happened to the other points? Arthur's friends laughed and nodded in agreement. The boys thought they were lying and their parents were psychotic.

This led to a discussion of report cards. Here Arthur's friends were unanimous. Parents knew when report cards were coming and had very high expectations. If they were not met, there were lectures, expressions of disappointment, anger and punishments, inversely related to the grades. Parents compared report cards with other parents and did not want to be embarrassed.

The boys said they didn't show their report cards to their parents. They signed the report cards themselves. When there were letters from the school about poor performance, they destroyed them. When there were phone calls, they didn't report them if they could get away with it. Their parents did not know what happened to their children in school or in the world outside of school. The boys attributed this to parents not speaking English, working long hours, having only one adult at home, not knowing the neighbors, and a cultural divide between the Dominican Republic and the United States. Where Arthur and his friends had tight curfews, which when violated resulted in serious punishments, the boys said their parents gave up on curfews when they couldn't enforce them. Even in middle school, Leo came home after 3 a.m. In contrast, it was difficult to get away with bad behavior when Arthur's friends were growing up. The neighbors turned them in. Parents seemed to know about what they had done before they got home. This astounded the boys.

The boys' attitude toward school reminded Arthur and his friends of their own behavior at Hebrew school. They acted out; they cut school; they didn't do homework; they attempted to hide report cards; they didn't bring notes home, and when possible, they tore up letters. They dropped out as soon as possible after compulsory schooling ended with their Bar Mitzvahs. This was only in part because Hebrew school was boring. More important, it was irrelevant. It did not matter. They saw no connection between Hebrew school and their futures. They knew no one whose career prospects or life was better because he had gone to Hebrew school. In a very real sense, this is what Carlos and his friends were telling them. They did not know many people whose lives were better because of school. Even Leo's mom, who had completed a postsecondary degree, was still cleaning toilets at the airport. Carlos's older brother who had some college was doing the same job as his father. Theoretically, the boys knew education was important, but there were a paucity of real life examples of beneficiaries. Moreover, they could not imagine what a better life looked like in reality. When debriefing with Laura after one of the conversations, the boys talked about what Arthur's friends lives must be like. They thought the neighborhood Arthur grew up in was boring, and so was his job at Teachers College. They said if they had as much money as he did, which was imagined with more zeroes than the reality, they would be more "gangsta" and open a discoteca.

But to Arthur's friends, education was a lifeline. They didn't know any other way up and out.

* * *

One question was asked over and over again throughout the conversations between Arthur's friends and Leo's friends together, with Leo's friends alone, and with Arthur's friends alone.[1] If you strip away the ethnic differences and the passage of 40 years, is the neighborhood the same or is it different? At the beginning, Juan Carlos said it was the same. In the end everyone agreed it was different. Perhaps it was Juan Carlos who described the changes and the continuities most thoughtfully, when he said, "Take away the music; take away the graffiti; take away the gates . . . take away the drugs and shootings and all that stuff [and] instead of me, Leo, and Carlos on the corner, it's Jim and his friends . . . playing football."

It was a poignant observation, but the stories of Leo and Arthur suggest that the differences between Creston Avenue now and then are simply not a matter of "take aways," but also "add ins." If all the things that Juan Carlos enumerated were to disappear, what would still be missing from the boys' lives is the belief Arthur and his friends shared that all things were possible and they had in their hands the means to achieve them. The lives of children on Creston Avenue then and now are profoundly different. When Arthur and his friends lived in the old neighborhood, Creston Avenue families were on the lower rungs of the middle-class ladder and the mechanisms for propelling youngsters upward were powerful. Today, the "old neighborhood" is isolated—disconnected from the middle class, and the means of mobility are broken.

The neighborhood is isolated linguistically. The residents do not speak the language of middle-class America, and middle-class America does not speak their language. According to 2007 U.S. Census Bureau data from the American Community Survey,[2] 68% of the residents in the 16th U.S. Congressional district, which includes the Creston Avenue neighborhood, do not speak English at home or on the streets, as Laura and Arthur observed. In fact, a third of the adult residents (34%) reported that they do not speak English "very well." Spanish is now the language of the "old neighborhood," and Miriam's experience shows just how difficult that makes finding a nonminimum wage job, even with a postsecondary degree.

The neighborhood is isolated racially. The residents of the 16th Congressional District are primarily Hispanic and Black (95%) in contrast to the nation, which is overwhelmingly White (74%). In the United States, where racial discrimination, segregation, and fear of people of color remain realities, this separates Creston Avenue and its children from the majority population. In fact, the rising concentration of people of color permit White America to view the entire neighborhood and its residents as "the other," "those people," less than themselves and undesirable.

Even at Teachers College, which is a very liberal community with students of color constituting more than 40% of its enrollment, seeing Leo and his friends in the hallways or at the president's community parties invariably brought wary looks and continuing scrutiny. For instance, a colleague told Laura that things had recently gone missing in her office and urged her to keep an eye on Leo, Juan Carlos, and Carlos. She said if she saw those "Black teenagers" walking down the halls of TC, she would call security.

Arthur and Laura were appalled, but the boys said they expected this. It was what they experienced when they looked for jobs, when they worked for Caucasian employers, when they had White teachers, whenever they found themselves in White America. Because of their skin color and accents, they felt they were treated as less able, less trustworthy, and less human. In contrast, Arthur and his friends were the same color as the majority of Americans.

The neighborhood is isolated economically. It is poor. In 2007, 43% of the families with children under the age of 18 in the 16th Congressional District lived below the poverty line, and the median household income was $23,291.

Leo's mom worked full-time, but the most money she ever earned was $7.00 an hour, or $13,440 a year. This was well below the poverty threshold of $18,307 a year for a family of four.[3] Each month Miriam and her three children survived in New York City on $1,120 before taxes. Poverty dictated the lives her family led, including where they lived, the schools they could attend, the food they ate, the legal services they had access to, and the health care they received.

The most common jobs in the neighborhood today are in the low-pay and low-education service industries (36%), as was the case with Leo's and Carlos's parents. In today's global economy, the jobs that Arthur's and his friends' parents had that paid a wage sufficient to support a family have disappeared, gone with their industries to other countries.

The current residents' futures are not promising because the fastest growing occupations in the country between 2006 and 2016, according to the U.S. Department of Labor, will be in the professions that require postsecondary education, and the service industries,[4] which pay salaries insufficient to support a family. Middle-class jobs are out of reach for most of the residents of the neighborhood today. Only 16% have earned two-year college degrees or higher, versus 34% for the country, a requirement for entering a professional career.[5]

Miriam's story makes clear just how difficult it is to get a better job living on Creston Avenue today. The primary source for job leads for her and her neighbors were other residents, who tended to be most knowledgeable about low-paying jobs. Finding jobs outside the neighborhood was problematic because few residents have cars and long commutes and long hours at work limit the amount of time that can be spent searching. The cost of transportation for a job search was also prohibitive for Miriam. When she decided to learn English as a means of improving her job possibilities, the same obstacles came into play.

The combination of low levels of education for residents and low-paying jobs has been devastating for the neighborhood, particularly when combined with the nation's current economic condition, which is closing businesses and eliminating jobs. It spurred the growth of illegal jobs. The most lucrative career in the neighborhood appeared to be dealing drugs, but the reality is that only the drug dealers at the top of the pyramid make large sums of money.[6] Those at the bottom on average earn less than minimum wage and have a greater likelihood of arrest and physical harm. Whether cause or effect or both, gangs spread rapidly, and the violence that drugs and gangs produced kept the middle class away from the neighborhood except as consumers. The police force and courts became less a vehicle for protecting the neighborhood than another source for generating fear and violence. Lisandro's arrest and trial demonstrated these realities as did the failure of the police to assist Leo when he was attacked, or to aid Miriam when she tried to retrieve Leo's possessions.

This situation in turn discouraged new businesses with higher paying jobs from coming to the neighborhood, and encouraged existing businesses to leave.

The neighborhood is also isolated educationally. Forty-two percent of the residents of the 16th Congressional District over the age of 24 have not completed high school. This means they lack the skills and knowledge needed to function socially in middle-class America or to qualify for middle-class jobs.

In short, Creston Avenue is isolated from the American middle class—linguistically, racially, economically, and educationally. Its residents do not speak the language of the middle class, nor does the middle class speak their language. They are not the same race as the middle class, and racial discrimination remains a reality in America. They do not have middle-class jobs or the prospect of getting them. And their educations disqualify them from entering the middle class.

* * *

The mechanisms for social mobility—families, mentors/role models, neighbors, and schools—which were so effective for Arthur and his friends no longer work. The family has diminished in impact. Parents are able to spend less time with their children than in Arthur's day. Today, 60% of all families with children under the age of 18 in the 16th Congressional District are headed by a single mother. As a result, the average child has only one parent at home and that parent is required to work to support the family. Children are more independent than when Arthur and his friends lived in the neighborhood, as the differences with curfew practices of the two generations illustrate.

Moreover, limited education and lack of experience in middle-class jobs makes it difficult for parents to counsel their children regarding schooling and careers, to be an advocate for their children in school, or to understand what their children are doing in school. Despite the lectures of Carlos's father or Leo's mother on the importance of doing well in school, they lacked the time, expertise, and language skills to turn their admonitions into practice for their children. This was not the case with Arthur and his friends.

This is compounded by the fact that a much larger number of parents than in Arthur's day are "hyphenated." They live in two worlds. While they reside in the "neighborhood," their futures remain in the Dominican Republic. They came to the United States not to live here permanently, but to earn enough money to build a home and a good life in the Dominican Republic. Their visits home are frequent, and many of their families and closest friends continue to live in the Dominican Republic. In this sense, their focus is more on achieving a Dominican dream than the traditional American dream.

When Arthur and his friends lived in the neighborhood, the parents did not have the choice of living in two worlds, though they may have yearned to do so. The ties to their countries of origin were involuntarily and painfully severed. They were robbed of the relatives and worlds they left behind. This meant the only future they had was in the United States, and the only dream possible was for their children to make it in this country.

Role models who demonstrated what "making it" looked like and the path to follow in order to make it have disappeared over the years, the result of White flight and fair housing laws—which made it illegal to exclude people of color from living in neighborhoods with majority populations of comparable educations and incomes. The doctors, teachers, and other professionals who once lived in the neighborhood are now gone. The long line of brothers and sisters, who had gone to college and left the neighborhood for better lives, has also vanished. The most successful individuals on Creston Avenue today are the gang leaders, whom Leo deeply admired for the respect they engendered and the money, cars, and girls they had. Most had never finished high school and showed not how to make it to the middle class, but rather how to adapt to and become wealthy in the concentrated poverty of Creston Avenue.

Neighbors too are less potent than in the past. They are less willing to act in *loco parentis* for all sorts of reasons, but one is that the population on Creston Avenue is more mobile. Between 2000 and 2007, 55% of the residents of the 16th Congressional District relocated.[7] The result is that neighbors know each other and the neighborhood kids less well than in the past, so the experience that Arthur and his friends had of parents learning about their misdeeds even before they arrived home is unlikely to be repeated today.

The schools, which were engines of mobility when Arthur and his friends lived on Creston Avenue, now prepare children to continue to live lives of poverty. They are underfunded. When Leo attended elementary school, his school received roughly $10,000 less *per child* compared to a suburban elementary school just 15 miles away. Less money translates into poorly paid teachers and overcrowded classrooms. Leo's teachers at that time received an average of $30,000 less in annual salary than their peers in affluent suburban schools, and his high school had so many students that it had to begin serving lunch at 9:21 a.m. to accommodate them all.[8] This is a sharp contrast with the research finding that it costs 40% more to educate a poor child because of the poverty-related disadvantages they bring to the classroom.

There was also a mismatch between the backgrounds of teachers and the children they taught in the old neighborhood. Too few of the teachers Arthur and Laura met in the course of this study looked like the children they taught, lived in their students' neighborhood, spent time with their children's families, spoke the language their children's families spoke, or knew about their students' cultures. One teacher at Leo's elementary school complained that the Dominican kids she taught had no "culture." They didn't play tennis or go to summer camp. Instead, they spent their vacations visiting their native countries.

Leo's teachers on average were also less competent than their suburban peers. They were more likely not to have majored or even taken a minor in the subject area they taught, not to have been certified as teachers, or required emergency appointments to justify placing them in a classroom.

They also had higher turnover rates. Research shows that teachers become more effective as they acquire experience in the classroom over the first 3 years. The fact that teachers in low-income urban schools have high attrition rates ensures that poor kids, who need the strongest teachers, are continually taught by rookies.

These schools had low expectations for their children. This was perhaps captured best at a neighborhood middle school graduation Arthur and Laura attended. In low-income neighborhoods, these tend to be as grand as the high school and college versions because for most of the children this is the last graduation they will have. They will drop out before completing high school. At this graduation, a banner was stretched across the room, proclaiming "No Dream Too Small." This was so appalling and blatant a dismissal of the children as to be laughable. Rather than telling them as Arthur and his friends were told that anything was possible, that no dream is too big, these kids were being told that however little they hoped for was sufficient and the less they dreamed of achieving, the better their dream.

Sometime later, Arthur visited with the principal of one of the neighborhood schools. She told him that all of the schools around hers were on the state list of failing schools. She reported that her's barely made it above the cut each year. Then with a big smile she said, "I am so proud." The bottom line for this principal is that the problem was the kids, not the schools, and her school was doing better than the others.

These schools were violent and dangerous places, mirroring the neighborhood. At Leo's high school different gangs controlled different floors, making it risky for him to attend his English classes because they were on a floor run by a rival gang.

The result is what one would expect. Fewer than half of all students graduate from high school in the "old neighborhood." During the course of this study, the elementary school, which served Arthur and his friends so well, was closed for the low quality of its performance.

Leo and his friends should have been furious at what was being done to them, but they weren't in part because they had never had the chance to attend a school of quality to compare their experience with[9] and because they didn't believe in the connection between education and their futures. For these reasons, it seemed absurd to them that Arthur's father would go crazy over a few points on a report card or Barry didn't cut classes or take a day off, or Debby did her homework every day, or Jim showed up for tests. Leo and the others knew education had theoretical value, but they did not see its relevance in practice.

For example, Leo said in a decade he imagined he would have a "house far from the neighborhood," be a "professional of something," have a wife with a high school diploma who made him "proud of what she work[ed] at," own cars, help his family, and have a "good education," including college. In the very next breath, Leo said he had not been in school in a long while, attended school that day, but did not go to class. Instead he had sex under the stairs.

There was a yawning chasm between what he wanted and what he did, a disconnect between what he knew and how he acted. He understood the theory of education and social mobility; he didn't practice it.

In the end what all of this adds up to is the fact that the children who grew up with Arthur had linguistic, racial, economic, and educational advantages, and the human and institutional capital to make mobility possible. Leo's generation did not.

PART IV

REVIVING
THE AMERICAN
DREAM

The Anomalies

Juan Carlos and Carlos, final year of college

Laura: Why do you think you made it to college?
Juan Carlos: For one, my own will and character; my family morals, which distinguished me from many people in the streets, and morals that I believed kept me from going over the edge in the streets; visiting Aneudys and seeing firsthand the pain his mother went through; the loss of friends, etc. I feel that the message here is that a good mentor can save lives and while that is true there is so much more . . . which contributed to my success. There was not one intervention in my case, I was fortunate enough to bump into many eye openers and opportunities.

Summer 2009

123

K NOCK ON ANY APARTMENT DOOR on Creston Avenue and the person who answers is likely to know many Leos—relatives, friends, and neighbors, who have lived lives with too little education, too much violence, and tragic consequences.

More unusual today are reports of the success stories, the anomalies, the neighborhood children who graduated from high school and went to college. This is a snapshot of two of them, Juan Carlos and Carlos, who were Leo's best friends. They are kids who managed to avoid the very real dangers of going to jail or being killed. The question is why, and what lessons can be learned from their experiences?

JUAN CARLOS

In many respects, Juan Carlos's story is much the same as Leo's. When Arthur and Laura met him, Juan Carlos, who had been born in the Dominican Republic in 1986, was 15 years old and already a major clothes horse. He had been a member of the AKs (All Korrupt gang) and was now a Latin King. He idolized gang drug dealers who had the glamour, respect, money, cars, and women Juan Carlos wanted. They taught him how to handle a gun, introduced him to drugs, and gave him money for running odd jobs. Juan Carlos was smart, quick with his hands, and unwilling to be disrespected, so although he was younger than the leaders, he was readily embraced by them.

They taught him how to make a quick hundred bucks by selling crack. Juan Carlos couldn't remember a time when he didn't know about drugs, or that the people on his corner were always selling drugs. There were drug spots on virtually every block from Burnside all the way to Fordham Road. The dilapidated building near Fordham Road was a crack house, and the little park on Burnside and Creston was a haven for junkies.

The AKs taught Juan that people earned spots by garnering respect and gaining reputations for being tough and having the capacity to hurt people who challenged them. To show him how to make his hundred, they took Juan to an abandoned warehouse in downtown Manhattan, introduced him to a dealer, who sold two bundles of crack, each containing 11 bags, for $550. Juan was told dealers put the bundles between the cheeks of their asses in case the cops showed up. He was given a place to stand. A spotter, he was shown, served as lookout, pointing out whom to sell to and whom not to. The first bundle sold in less than an hour, and the second moved even more quickly.

Juan decided he was not cut out to be a drug dealer. He was disgusted by the filth of the warehouse, repulsed by the desperation of the buyers, and afraid of getting caught. He didn't like where dealers had to keep the drugs either. But he certainly did not follow the straight and narrow.

Like Leo, Juan Carlos was doing poorly in school. He had attended three different high schools. He was expelled from the first for hitting a security guard, who he thought was disrespecting him. At the second, he cut school more than he attended, was a habitué of hooky parties, and managed to accumulate one academic credit by the conclusion of his freshman year. At the third, he was suspended three times for misbehaving on a field trip, throwing a bottle of urine at a classmate, and coming to school high. After the third incident, Juan was told there would be no more chances.

He wasn't sure he cared. School was boring, and he just wanted out. Juan Carlos wasn't sure what difference school made anyway. His sister was just a few credits short of earning a 2-year college degree, yet she worked in a Pennsylvania factory packing chickens. That didn't compare with the life of a Latin King. Juan Carlos was one of the few Latin Kings still in school when he was in ninth grade, but given his academic performance, this appeared only temporary.

* * *

He was headed in the same direction as Leo. If anything, his record was even worse. But this is where their two paths diverge. Juan Carlos had a series of assets Leo lacked.

He had two parents, two people to watch over him, two people to nurture him, and two incomes at home. Though neither of his parents had completed high school—his mother had an 8th-grade education and his stepfather completed 10th grade—both parents were entrepreneurs.

His stepdad Alejandro, who grew up in a privileged family in Mexico, came to the United States to make money. Speaking only Spanish, the only job he could get was as a dishwasher, but he was hardworking and learned quickly. He moved up the kitchen hierarchy from dishwashing to prepping to cooking within a year. Other cooking jobs followed, paying as much as $700 a week.

Soon, he wanted his own business. The opportunity came when a friend decided to sell his pizza joint on 183rd and Morris Avenue, a block west of Creston. Alejandro bought it and opened a restaurant.

In the end, the restaurant failed. Alejandro was forced to sell it at a loss of $50,000, owing to an accident which left him unable to cook. In the years after, he sold fruit on the streets, worked at restaurants, and was employed as a cook in Pennsylvania until he got deported to Mexico for his illegal status. Juan Carlos was 21 years old at the time.

Juan Carlos's mom, Florinda, was one of 13 children, who had to leave school after the sixth grade because her parents could not afford for her to continue. She completed the next 2 years of schooling by radio.

Over the years, she sought out educational opportunities. She took sewing lessons in the Dominican Republic for as long as she could afford them so she could make some money as a seamstress. She enrolled in a 2-week home healthcare worker program in the United States, which enabled her to get a job in the field. Being part of a two-parent family with the support of her husband made this more feasible. She doesn't speak much English, but when she wanted to become a U.S. citizen, she had Juan Carlos grill her on the sample questions, memorized the answers in English, and passed the exam.

Juan Carlos viewed Flor as smart and as someone who knew how to make money. Because of health problems, she was unemployed at the time of this study, but received unemployment payments of approximately $250 biweekly. She also had worked as a cab driver, making roughly $60 a day weekdays and a hundred on weekends. In addition, she charged a boarder $100 a week for a room in her apartment, and when Juan Carlos's stepfather moved out, she asked Juan Carlos to pitch in and pay for expenses, using the money he earned from his part-time job.

Both parents lectured their son regularly about doing better than they did, like most of the parents encountered on Creston Avenue, but Juan Carlos said he was never sure what they wanted. He put it this way, "My mom is always talking about how she ain't nobody. . . . She has to clean up an apartment and take care of kids and listen to orders by someone who is given her services by the government." He suspects she doesn't want him working in McDonald's or the supermarket, but rather in an office in a suit. Juan Carlos says his mom never told him this, but it comes without saying.

If his parents' message was not explicit, his parents' behavior was. For Juan Carlos, they served as examples of the power of ambition, imagination, hard work, and an individual's capacity to create a better life. He did not want to disappoint them as the oldest male in the family.

* * *

Beyond his parents, Juan Carlos had other adults in his life who looked out for him. They included teachers in middle school and high school, like Mr. Abadia, Mr. Saltz, Mr. Nichols, and Ms. Dhakkar, who took an interest in him, conveyed high expectations, spoke of his potential, and made themselves available outside of class.

Ms. Dhakkar, Juan's high school global studies teacher, never stopped asking him, why? She was demanding and a superb motivational speaker, telling students "If you can pass my class, then you can pass the Regents" (the statewide test required for graduation in her subject area). But what was most important to Juan was the time Ms. Dhakkar, who was born in Somalia, spent talking with him and other students outside of class. She shared personal experiences that he could relate to, like her struggles adapting to a new country and being discriminated against because of the color of her skin. One day, he told Ms. Dhakkar that he planned to graduate from high school in 4 years. She looked at him and said, "I don't think that you can do it." Startled by her response, Juan Carlos told her that he was going to take night school, Saturday school, and summer school to make up for his missing credits. If he passed all of his classes, then he could do it. "Let's make a bet," she challenged him. "If you graduate in 4 years, I'll take you out to lunch, on me." He went to his next class, determined to prove Ms. Dhakkar wrong.

There was the principal of the Heritage School, Juan Carlos's third and final secondary school, who took a chance on Juan Carlos, admitting him, counseling him, and disciplining him for infractions, somehow imposing clear standards and managing to keep Juan Carlos in school and on a path that led to graduation.

But one person stood out for Juan Carlos, his Heritage School karate instructor named Rachel "Rocky" Rivera, or "Sensei" to her students. She was his mentor, introducing Juan Carlos to a subject he loved and using that to motivate him to perform. A stocky 50-year-old Puerto Rican woman, Sensei was born and raised in a rough neighborhood in Brooklyn. She was a Master in Goju, Taekwondo, and Vee Jitsu. When she yelled, "Let's go," her students scrambled to do laps around the gym. The laps were followed by *katas*, kicks, defense moves, and mat work. At the end of class the students lined up and said, "*Arigato, gosaimasu, Sensei.*" No one left until Sensei said, "*Go Kuro San*" and the lead student announced that class was dismissed.

Sensei, who had not completed college, taught him to love martial arts and to respect the discipline and honor associated with them. She spoke to him about growing up on the streets, introduced him to her successful students who were in the navy or in college, took him to weekend karate tournaments, yelled at him when she had to, and punished him in class when it was necessary. But she always ended their arguments with a hug and said she really cared. The more Juan Carlos got into karate, the less time he spent with his friends in the Bronx.

One day, Juan Carlos ran into Sensei in the cafeteria and she asked him if this was his lunch period. He said yes. But later, she checked with his guidance counselor and found that Juan had not only been cutting that day, but that he was also failing most of his classes. Sensei prohibited him from going for his karate promotion to yellow belt until he was passing all of his classes, explaining that he needed to be disciplined inside and outside of the *dojo* (karate school). He also had to do 500 extra pushups in karate for cutting classes. Juan Carlos didn't know if he felt worse about missing his promotion, doing 500 pushups, or disappointing Sensei. But he promised himself he would do better.

This contrasted sharply with Juan's experience at his two prior high schools, where security guards watched him leave school early to go to hookies or allowed him to play dominoes in the cafeteria even though they knew he was cutting.

Juan Carlos was almost expelled from the Heritage School for coming to school stoned. He and his friends smoked marijuana in a nearby park before school. When Sensei saw his red eyes, she asked him, "Have you been smoking?" "No." She knew better and reported it to the principal. They arranged a meeting with his parents and discussed the possibility of filing a petition to classify him as a "Person In Need of Supervision," which would have put his future in the hands of a family court judge. In the end, Juan Carlos was only suspended from school and warned that if he messed up again, he would get kicked out.

He changed his ways and graduated on time. After the graduation ceremony, Sensei gave him a present. He unwrapped it and teared up. It was a kicking pad. Sensei smiled at Juan Carlos and told him, "You deserve it. You worked hard and I'm proud of you."

He found Ms. Dhakkar and told her, "You owe me lunch. I knew I would win the bet." She congratulated him and added with a satisfied look, "Reverse psychology. I knew you would do it if I told you that you couldn't."

In sum, Juan Carlos had the right high school. Unlike Kennedy, where Leo had enrolled, Heritage, established to demonstrate that disadvantaged kids deserved and could have public schools as good as those found in the suburbs, was small and knew its students by name, not by number. Its standards and expectations were high. Postsecondary education was expected and the support to make that possible—college counseling, free SAT courses, and college visits—was provided. Its faculty and staff worked with students in and out of class. The school had external financial support to provide these services. Its principal believed people sometimes "need a second, third, fourth, or fifth chance." All of the students in the first graduating class went on to college except for the few who joined the military. Subsequent classes mirrored this pattern.

* * *

Juan Carlos also had the benefit of enrichment experiences outside of school. One day, before Juan Carlos transferred to Heritage, he and Leo were talking about their friends—nearly everyone they knew had dropped out of school and done little with their lives. Juan Carlos decided he wanted something better. He would graduate from high school, but had no desire to go to college.

Outward Bound, an expeditionary learning program, was a turning point. Shortly after that conversation with Leo, he had seen a camping trip advertised at Roosevelt High School and decided to register because he liked trying new things. It was a 2-week trip with six other students to the Adirondacks in upstate New York. It was the first time Juan Carlos had seen a forest, the first time he slept in a tent, the first time he canoed, the first time he lived without indoor bathroom facilities. Outward Bound required all participants to spend 24 hours alone with just a package of crackers and cheese, and a pad and pen to reflect on their lives and where they wanted to go. Juan Carlos wrote about graduating from high school.

Outward Bound was one of the hardest but most rewarding experiences of his life. When he came back, he hugged his mom and stepfather and told them how much he loved them and how thankful he was for everything they did for him. He found himself grateful for little things like toilets, electricity, and his mom's cooking. He also returned with a renewed commitment to completing high school.

Juan Carlos told Leo all about the trip. He didn't get it and said, "That sounds wack." Juan Carlos tried not to let his reaction bother him, even though it did. "I just gotta think about what I learned and do good in high school," Juan Carlos told himself. He knew that he needed to get away from his friends in the Bronx if he wanted to graduate from high school.

The second enrichment experience was a field trip to Vassar College during his junior year at Heritage. Juan Carlos and his classmates sat in on classes, spoke to Vassar students, and spent the night in the dorms to see what campus life was all about. When he got home, Juan told his friends, "College is butter! I wish I had gone on that trip my freshman year instead of junior year." He decided to attend college, and Juan's teachers reinforced his decision.

The third enrichment experience was much like Arthur's visit to his classmate's Park Avenue apartment. As the research on the old neighborhood progressed, Juan Carlos and his friends spent increasing amounts of time at Teachers College. He met people who worked there. He saw a slice of life that was not traditionally open to children on Creston Avenue, a part of the world he did not know existed. Through the connections he made at Teachers College, he was able to attend parties at the president's home and he got a job working in the president's office. If Outward Bound motivated Juan Carlos to complete high school and the Vassar visit encouraged him to go to college, the personal connections he made at Teachers College helped him gain access to resources that could help him get to college. They also helped him bridge the gap between the theory and the reality of social mobility.

Equally powerful to Juan Carlos was the prison visit with Aneudys. He never wanted to go to jail, to hurt the people in his life who loved him. He never wanted to be in a situation where his freedom was denied and he was forced to do what others told him.

*   *   *

What made it possible for Juan Carlos to go to college was counseling, finding the right school, financial aid, and a transition program. After deciding he wanted to attend college, Juan did some Internet research and found Briarcliffe College, a small vocational school on Long Island. He wanted to live away from home, so he was happy to learn the school had dorms, actually a budget motel about a mile away from the campus.

He was convinced that was the school he would attend until he met Cindy, who worked for the Harlem Center for College Outreach. Two days a week, she came to the Heritage School to acquaint students with a world that was alien to most, help them navigate the college paperwork labyrinth, and assist them individually to find and get admitted to a college. She worked with Juan Carlos on college applications as well as completing a New York State Higher Education Opportunity

Program (HEOP) application, a program offering financial support to low-income students judged to have potential to do well in college.

In addition to Briarcliffe, Juan visited Mount Saint Mary College for an HEOP interview. He reported back to Cindy that he liked the school "because it's small like Heritage and they have new dorms. Plus it's close to home, so I could visit on the weekends." During his interview he told the Mount Saint Mary staff members that he had gone from a 50% GPA his freshman year to an 83% in his senior year. He hoped the improvement would be enough to be one of the 10 out of 100 applicants chosen for the HEOP program, and by dint of personality, he was.

Two days after graduation, Juan Carlos put his bags in his mom's car and drove to Mount Saint Mary College for the HEOP summer program. All HEOP students had to go through an intensive 6-week summer "academic boot camp," which served as a transition from his life in the Bronx to college. On Monday morning, Juan Carlos and the nine other HEOP students had to be at breakfast by 7:35 a.m. Classes, which lasted 7 hours a day, began at 8. Dinner was at 5:30 and mandatory tutoring began at 6 p.m. Curfew was 11 p.m. Juan Carlos spent most of his free time doing homework. By the second day, he hated it. He had never before studied so hard and didn't think he was going to make it. He nearly quit several times, but hung in. By the end of the program, Juan Carlos won most improved writer and couldn't wait for the school year to begin.

For freshman orientation, the school sponsored a boat trip around Manhattan. Juan Carlos looked at the other students; nearly all were White. His roommate, Rolando, was also Hispanic. But he felt out of place and wanted to go home. He stopped by the HEOP office to tell them of his decision. The director, Daniela, also a Dominican, confessed to feeling the same way at times. Being one of the few minority staff members, she felt like everyone was looking at her. "That's exactly how I feel," Juan Carlos said. They talked about how she adjusted over time and how he could do the same. He promised her he'd give it another try.

Juan Carlos was elected freshman class president during his first term at college, but by the end of the semester he was scared; if he got less than a C average or failed any of his classes, he could be dismissed from the HEOP program. He had stayed up all night studying for his math exam, didn't have a topic for his final English paper, hadn't opened his *Introduction to Management* book for the final, and still had to take an accounting exam, a class in which he had gotten a "D" on the midterm. His academic advisor calmed him down and stoked him up. Juan Carlos barely slept the next 3 nights, but ended up with a 3.0 GPA his first semester in college.

Juan Carlos packed his stuff for the 6-week winter break and got a ride back to the city. When he stepped out of the car, he felt like a celebrity. Even if no one else knew that he had just come back from "The Mount," it felt good to be one of the few from the block to go to college.

*   *   *

In many ways Juan Carlos straddled two worlds once he started college. This was highlighted when he visited home during holidays. For example, during Christmas break, the first person he called was Leo, who told him the latest, "I got mad-girls." Leo bragged about all the hooky parties he had been to recently. Over the next 6 weeks, Juan Carlos and Leo were together almost 24 hours a day at hooky parties dancing, drinking, and trying to get with girls. "It was like some kind of ghetto vacation," Juan Carlos joked. He wanted to squeeze in a semester's worth of Bronx partying into 6 weeks.

During that 6 weeks, Juan Carlos returned to the rules of the neighborhood. For example, at one of the parties he attended, Juan Carlos's friends "ran a train," on a friend's girlfriend. She gave oral sex to four guys before having sex with her boyfriend. The next day, she called Juan Carlos and told him, "That's kinda messed up what they did to me." "What are you talking about?" he said. "You were the one who went to the bathroom with them." He had heard stories about girls who messed with guys and then claimed that they took advantage of them because the girls were drunk. At the party, she was the one grabbing the guys, not the other way around. He needed to be careful. He didn't want to ruin his future over some "chicken head."

It wouldn't have been the old neighborhood if there weren't fights. On New Year's Eve, some guy punched his friend Jose, who threatened to get a gun but ended up doing nothing. Juan Carlos was disappointed in him. "I am not the most gangsta cat on the block," Juan Carlos said, "but if someone punches me I don't care who it is. I am swinging back."

The same sort of thing happened a few days later. Juan's friend Diego, who was drunk, threw a bottle at a guy named Marcos, who wanted revenge. Diego told Juan Carlos that he didn't want to fight and was willing to apologize. Juan Carlos did not say anything but thought, "Where have you been your whole life? Have the streets not taught you anything?" As Juan Carlos saw it, if Marcos and his friends were going to jump Diego, the only option Diego had was to get a weapon and defend himself. Juan Carlos was also friends with Marcos, so he tried convincing him not to jump Diego and instead fight him "one-deep." Marcos refused and told Juan Carlos, "He hit me with a bottle. There's no one-deep now." Juan Carlos respected what he said. Even though he had been away at school and in a different world, he still knew that those were the rules of the block.

*   *   *

By the end of the break, Juan Carlos was ready to go back to school, but being home made him realize how much he loved his neighborhood. He missed hearing Latino music and it felt good to be around people who understood him. But being home also reminded him of what he disliked about the Bronx. He hated the drugs, the stabbings and the shootings, and the way the cops treated him. The graffiti and filth were more apparent after being away. Juan Carlos was glad to be one of the few to get out, and he was determined to bring others with him, starting with Carlos and Leo.

In the end, Juan Carlos found living in two worlds, Mount Saint Mary's and the Bronx, and fitting into neither, impossible. After 2 years, the personal problems he faced back home—specifically Leo's death and the health problems that his mom had—as well as the racism he perceived at the college drove him back to the city. He got a job at Teachers College, transferred to Baruch College of the City University of New York, and moved back to the Bronx. He has no regrets about beginning his college career at "The Mount" because he enjoyed college campus life, but is also happy to be finishing his degree in New York City.

CARLOS

Carlos was a very different kid than his friends Leo and Juan Carlos. He didn't belong to a gang, concluding it was too much work, and even if membership was designed to protect you, belonging to a gang got you into other fights. The big plus he saw was that girls liked guys in gangs, but he was too shy to take much advantage of that anyway.

Carlos did not seek out trouble, but if a friend needed help, Carlos would be there for him. But he was more inclined to use humor to dodge problems than his fists to engage it. In contrast to Leo and Juan Carlos, who were obviously streetwise, Carlos seemed innocent, naïve, and a little goofy.

All of this said, it was extremely unlikely that a youngster growing up on Creston Avenue could avoid trouble entirely. Sometimes trouble found Carlos. One day, he and a friend were yanked off the subway by a group of teenagers. They stabbed Carlos six times, beat him with a metal pipe, and kicked him repeatedly in the head and face. His friend sustained a greater number of stab wounds.

Carlos was very fortunate in that his thick leather jacket absorbed many of the cuts and reduced the depth of others. His friend required more than 50 stitches. The explanation for the attack appeared to be Carlos's friend, who while not a gang member, was friendly with one. He thought the attackers were members of a rival gang. Carlos recovered at home, while his friends went to Harlem to look for his attackers. When they didn't find them, they jumped someone else who might have been part of the same gang.

*   *   *

The similarities between Carlos and Leo and Juan Carlos were these: Carlos too had been born in the Dominican Republic. Like Juan Carlos, his parents had not graduated from high school, completing eight grades each, and worked in factories. He attended poor schools as Leo and Juan Carlos did, before finding Heritage.

Carlos went to Park West High School, which enrolled more than 2,000 students and was located in midtown Manhattan. It was a dismal place academically, and dangerous as well. More students dropped out than graduated the year Carlos entered. Only 11 students graduated with academic diplomas. The high school was closed the year after Carlos graduated.

Violence was omnipresent. Fights between rival gangs happened almost daily. Even if not in a gang, students were not safe. For example, Carlos's sneakers were stolen. He had put his new Michael Jordan's, which he loved and other students seemed to envy, in a gym locker. When the class ended, he found his locker had been smashed and the $200 shoes gone.

Carlos hated Park West, but he did not want to transfer to his local high school, Roosevelt, where Juan Carlos had been enrolled, because he thought he would do much worse.

Like his friends, Carlos cut school often and had a very poor academic record. He started cutting once a week during his freshman year, but once a week turned into twice a week and by his sophomore year, Carlos was cutting almost every day. He'd show up in the middle of first period and then would sneak out after third period when attendance was taken. Sometimes he went to hooky parties, but often he just hung out down the street with other Park West students.

At this point, Carlos was more likely to drop out of school than to go to college. What changed his trajectory were two people. While he had several of the advantages that Juan Carlos shared—two parents at home, exposure to middle-class life, financial aid, the right college, and a transition program—what mattered most were his father, who pushed him through high school, and Juan Carlos, who pulled him into college.

Like Meyer Levine, Carlos's dad Ismael had a dreaded, never-ending education lecture. On the day he found out that Carlos was failing a class, Ismael, desperate for his son to do better in school and graduate from a U.S. high school, spoke to Carlos slowly and dramatically in Spanish, never once yelling. Ismael told him,

> You need to listen to your teacher, even if she is ugly and you don't like her. She is like a second parent to you. . . . I may not be the most educated man, and I may not always use the right words, but I know what is best for my son. God gave you a nose and eyes to sense if something is wrong. And if one of your friends ever wants you to get involved in something bad, just tell him that you can't and walk away. . . . You have to do your part. . . . You need to use the intelligence that God gave you. . . . I want you home at 9:30. This is coming from your dad who loves you and adores you. Do we understand each other?

Carlos nodded.

*   *   *

Carlos loved and respected his father more than anyone else. Ismael acted like a father figure to all of Carlos's friends. He was constantly lecturing Carlos, and if his friends happened to be there, then they got it too. It was strikingly different from Leo's relationship with his own father. Leo was more afraid of Carlos's father than his own mother. One time Leo was with friends who were smoking pot in the entryway of Carlos's apartment building. When Ismael walked by, Leo froze in fear at the thought of Ismael thinking he smoked too. The possibility of disappointing him terrified Leo. So he avoided him.

Ismael worked long hours at a factory in New Jersey, waking at 2 a.m. each morning, commuting an hour-and-a-half to his job, working from

6 a.m. to 3:30 p.m., and then returning home. He was a loving father, who doted on Carlos, his youngest child, and was determined that he stay on the straight and narrow.

On Saturday mornings, Carlos sometimes went to the intramural sports club at his school. One Saturday, a PTA meeting was scheduled at the same time on the topic of how to stop students from using marijuana in the hallways. After the meeting, Ismael went to the gymnasium to find his son. He saw the intramural instructor and introduced himself. Ismael asked if Carlos was behaving well in school. The instructor said "Yes." Carlos had always been one of his quietest and best-behaved students. Ismael then asked, "How is my son doing in his classes?" Luckily for Carlos, the coach only knew about homeroom and gym class. He was doing well in both. Ismael thanked him for his time and apologized for bothering him. "I love my son very much," he explained, "and I worry about him." The two shook hands and the coach assured him that he could talk to him anytime.

*   *   *

Park West sometimes sent automatic phone messages telling parents that their children were not in school, but this was not a concern to Carlos because his parents didn't speak English. His father's work schedule meant he couldn't talk to teachers during the week, and Carlos's mom felt too sick to travel 45 minutes to his school. So even though his parents asked about school, and his dad continued with his education lectures, Carlos failed most of his classes his sophomore year.

During the winter of what should have been Carlos's senior year, the school sent home a notice about his excessive absences. Carlos's niece, who was living with the family at the time, translated the letter for his father. He assumed that there was a mistake because "Carlos wouldn't miss school." But Carlos's niece, who had already dropped out of high school and knew how easy it was to cut, insisted that Carlos was missing school. When Carlos denied the absences, Ismael made an appointment during one of his days off to meet with a counselor.

At the meeting that Ismael did not tell Carlos he had scheduled, he learned Carlos had cut a lot of classes. He missed 14 days of school last month and 3 so far in the first 2 weeks of the current month.

The counselor sent for Carlos. While they waited, Ismael asked if Carlos had been behaving well in school. The counselor had not heard of any problems. Ismael was relieved.

A few minutes later Carlos sauntered into the room and stopped in his tracks when he saw his father. Ismael softly spoke,

Mi hijo, why aren't you going to school? Why aren't you doing your part? . . . *Mi hijo,* we are here in this country because there are many opportunities for those who do their part. In the United States you can do anything you want, but you have to do your part. I don't know if you feel less important because they are White and you have darker skin, but we are all human beings and you are equal to them. I brought you to the United States for more opportunities, and the counselors and the teachers are here to help you. So you should listen to them, just like you listen to me. You are a good son, docile and well-mannered, and the counselor told me that you don't have any problems in school, and I'm proud of you for that. But you have to do your part. You have to go to class and study.

Desperate to get out of that room, Carlos promised the counselor and his father that he would go to school, along with night school and Saturday school to make up for the missing credits, though he refused to continue attending a class he had already passed, which the school mistakenly assigned him to retake. For more than a month Carlos had been trying to get the school to correct its error.

The counselor reminded Ismael that report cards came out on the 23rd of the month. He asked, "Has Carlos shown you any of his report cards?" "No," Ismael responded. The counselor nodded knowingly. Ismael thought that Park West was a good school.

In the aftermath of the meeting, Carlos cut fewer classes because he felt humiliated in front of his father and wanted to graduate as soon as possible. In fact, that semester he passed his night school classes, Saturday classes, and received three credits from summer school. By the end of his 4th year at Park West, Carlos was 8 classes shy of graduating. In his 5th year, Carlos took a combination of day, night, and weekend classes and got his highest grade point average ever.

His one remaining requirement for graduation was a Saturday gym course. Carlos had missed two classes, which technically meant that he should have failed. He missed one when he overslept and another when he had to serve as translator for his mom at a doctor's appointment. Carlos went to school to pick up his report card and was very pleasantly surprised, shocked may be more accurate, to find he had passed all of his classes.

Carlos wasn't sure what he wanted to do after graduating. When he started high school, he had wanted to join the army and fly planes. But when the Iraq war began, the army no longer seemed so appealing. Carlos thought about getting a job as a security guard because he had gotten a security guard certificate. His friend from school promised him a job making $10 an hour. But Carlos had lost touch with that friend. He had thought about college but wasn't terribly motivated to go back to school. Plus, the college process seemed overwhelming. He didn't know where to begin. Instead, he stayed home most days taking care of his mom, who was ill with Parkinson's disease and high blood pressure. As soon as his dad came home from work around 7 p.m., Carlos was out the door, looking for Leo or his other friends.

*   *   *

This is where Juan Carlos, who was already enrolled at Mount Saint Mary's, enters the story. He had been bugging Leo and Carlos to visit him at school for months. Sometime in February, they accepted the invitation. When they arrived at the train station, about an hour and a half from the city, Juan Carlos picked them up and drove them to a small college campus with a big football field and brand new dorms. Juan Carlos proudly showed them the computer room on the first floor of the dorms. They played basketball in the recreation center, and they used Juan Carlos's guest pass to eat in the cafeteria. After dinner, they drank Coronas in his friend's room and got ready for a party. After, Carlos and Leo crashed in the lobby of the girls' dormitory. Leo spent most of Sunday in the computer room on the Internet chatting with girls. Carlos hung out with Juan Carlos and his friends.

College was more fun than Carlos had expected. The school had everything he needed—a basketball court, education, food, friends, and parties. By Monday both Carlos and Leo decided that they wanted to go to college.

Juan Carlos introduced them to Daniela, the director of the HEOP program. She encouraged Carlos to apply as soon as possible because most students had already turned in their applications months earlier. She told him how to fill out an HEOP application and urged him to send his SAT scores, college essay, and school transcripts as soon as possible. Carlos wasn't exactly sure what all that meant, but he would do his best to follow her instructions. She seemed like a nice lady, and he didn't want to let her down. Leo promised to start studying for his GED, and Daniela encouraged him to work on his English and Spanish.

Carlos wanted to follow in Juan Carlos's footsteps. He tried to get a transcript from Park West, which was a challenge at a school that was closing. The teacher who promised Carlos a reference was gone. And a counselor, recommended by Juan Carlos to help him fill out his college application, told Carlos that she didn't think he could apply to the HEOP program because he was not a citizen.

Carlos threw out his Mount Saint Mary application and applied to the City University of New York (CUNY). He tried to convince himself that going to CUNY was better than Mount Saint Mary College. But deep down, Carlos really wanted to go to Juan Carlos's school.

Leo's and Carlos's second trip to Juan Carlos's school was similar to the first. They slept on the floor of Juan Carlos's room, drank before going out to a night club, played basketball, and ate in the cafeteria using Juan Carlos's guest pass. When Carlos realized that he could eat as much as he wanted, he filled his plate to the max. Twice.

Leo vowed to get his GED, but back in the Bronx nothing changed. Hooky parties. Friends getting stabbed. Friends stabbing others. Fights with his mom and her boyfriend. Leo began spending more time at Juan Carlos's school than at home. When he was home, there was nothing to do. Even if there was nothing to do at the Mount, at least it was *tranquilo*. It felt like a vacation from all the stress in the Bronx.

*   *   *

Carlos had given up on attending the Mount until Juan Carlos stopped by the HEOP office. The director asked him why Carlos hadn't turned in his application yet. When Juan Carlos told her, "Because he's not a citizen," she said it didn't matter. He could still apply. When Carlos heard the good news, he filled out an application as fast as he could, got letters of recommendation and an incomplete transcript, the best his school could produce. The essay, one typed, double-spaced page, took him hours and hours.

For his interview, Carlos borrowed a dress shirt from his father and wore his nicest pair of pants. Daniela complimented him on how well he looked before the three HEOP representatives took turns asking Carlos why he wanted to go to their school and why they should accept him. Carlos did his best to answer their questions; Juan Carlos had coached him. "I like the small size of the school because students get more attention from professors. I think I would be a good student because. . . ." Carlos was painfully shy around adults he didn't know, and he fought the urge to look at the floor and make jokes. By the end of the interview, Carlos felt more relaxed, and all of the interviewers thought he was a nice young man. But not all of them were convinced he was a good match for the program. The program only had 10 slots and Carlos had one of the worst grade point averages, turned in one of the worst essays, and his SAT scores were in the bottom 3% of the nation.

The next week Daniela called Juan Carlos to her office to talk about Carlos. He told her the truth. Carlos deserved a chance. He had gone to a horrible high school where more students dropped out than graduated in 4 years. Despite the odds, Carlos had graduated and was one of the 3% of his class to have earned an academic diploma. He believed that given the chance, Carlos would do well. Plus Juan Carlos, whose opinion mattered because he was one of their biggest success stories, promised to look after his friend. His case was persuasive and despite serious doubts, the committee admitted Carlos.

Ismael could not have been prouder. Not only had his son graduated from high school in the United States, but he was going to college.

THE LESSONS

The bottom line is this: There is a dramatic disparity in high school graduation rates by race and income in America. By race, the high school dropout rate for Whites 18 to 24 years of age is 16%; for Blacks it is 24%; and for Hispanics it is 33%.[1] By income, young people 16 to 24 years of age in the lowest income quartile (17%) drop out at more than 5 times the rate of their peers in the highest income quartile (3%).[2]

The gap is even greater for college. Sixty-one percent of Whites 25 years old or older enrolled in college versus 48% of Blacks and 33% of Hispanics.[3] There is almost a 50-percentage point disparity between college attendance rates between the top income quartiles (71%) and bottom (22%).[4]

With regard to college graduation, 34% of Whites 25 years of age or older receive a baccalaureate or higher credential in contrast to 20% of Blacks and 13% of Hispanics.[5] By income, the gap is sevenfold between the highest income quartile (42%) and the lowest (6%).[6]

This means that for Juan Carlos and Carlos, the odds were a little better than one in five, coming from the nation's bottom income quartile and one in three being Hispanic that they would attend college. They beat the odds for several reasons.

- *They had mentors.* Arthur first recognized the importance of mentors during his research about 25 years ago. In the mid-1980s, when Arthur was president of Bradford College, he spent a week living at a low-income housing project in Lawrence, Massachusetts, one of the poorest cities in the United States, in order to better understand the low college attendance of poor youngsters. While there he spoke to the children and parents, largely single mothers, living in the complex.

He asked the moms what they wanted for their children. They gave the answers mothers usually give. They wanted their children to do well, be happy, and not get into trouble. When he asked them about college, their eyes went blank. He realized, he had asked them the equivalent of whether they expected their children to travel to Mars. They were not college people. College was outside their experience and expectations.

Their children didn't know anyone who had gone to college. As in the South Bronx of Leo, Carlos, and Juan Carlos, the most successful people in the neighborhood were gang leaders and drug dealers.

When Arthur returned to Bradford, he established a scholarship for a child living in the projects. The next fall, a student arrived from Lawrence. Arthur asked him if he had come to college because of the scholarship. He said he had come to Bradford because of the scholarship, but he had always planned to attend college.

Arthur had an epiphany. Much of his research had focused on the pathologies of poverty. He had ignored the anomalies, those youngsters who get to college in spite of the neighborhood, who somehow attend higher education rather than dealing drugs, being arrested, or getting killed. He concluded that the exceptions offered a very fertile ground for learning how to assist low-income children escape poverty.

With a Harvard doctoral student, Jana Nidiffer, he conducted a study of anomalies attending two very different colleges—Harvard and Bunker Hill Community College.[7] They interviewed 24 poor, first-generation college students. They discovered that the student stories were fundamentally the same. Arthur joked that it was like reading a series of books by the same B novelist. The stories, with one exception, all had the same plot. In every case, there had been a mentor—a person who steered the student from the neighborhood to college.

The mentors were remarkable. They had very little in common—ethnicity, educational level, socioeconomic status, vocation, or even their relationship with the student. They were relatives, neighbors, teachers, counselors, and other professionals. The only generalization that could be offered about them is that the later in life students encountered the mentor, the more likely he or she was to be highly educated, a nonrelative, and a professional, such as a therapist or social worker. What the mentors as a group shared were four characteristics. They were committed to the American Dream, believing that with hard work any child can succeed. They thought that education was the driver for success in the United States. They were bicultural, in the sense that they could understand both the cultures of poverty and middle-class life in America and what was required to make the journey from one to the other. And they believed they could make a difference in a child's life and were determined to do so.

Juan Carlos and Carlos each had strong mentors. For Juan Carlos, there were several teachers and counselors, particularly at the Heritage School. His martial arts instructor was especially important. They believed that he could not only graduate from high school, but also go to college. For Carlos, there was Juan Carlos. As noted earlier, his dad got him through high school, and Juan Carlos got him to college.

• *They had contact with the world outside the neighborhood.* Although this project immersed Arthur and Laura in the lives of Carlos and Juan Carlos, it also exposed Juan Carlos and Carlos to Arthur and Laura's worlds; to the Teachers College community, and to the people Arthur grew up with. The boys saw a more affluent, more educated slice of life and met people with different resources and experiences. This was reminiscent of both Arthur's conversations with the professionals who lived in the old neighborhood and his visit to John's apartment.

While the boys' experience ameliorated the isolation inherent in growing up on Creston Avenue, it was more like a study-abroad program in their own city than an immersion experience. Their experiences gave the boys glimpses of a different life, though they were not always certain of what they had seen.

In addition to being exposed to a different world, they had the necessary social connections to help them dip into that world if they chose to do so. Juan Carlos, for example, got a job at Teachers College and had an even richer experience with his extended exposure to Teachers College, though he certainly did not always like what he saw. Reflecting on all the factors that got him out of trouble and on a path to college, he said the institution of Teachers College was the least important. He said the visit with Aneudys was more significant in convincing him to stay clear of trouble. However, the fact that he had been given a chance at a job at the college played a big part in his social mobility. His experience highlights the value of work-related internships as vehicles for introducing low-income youngsters to the professional world. They are worthy of expanding, both for the youngsters and the professionals.

The bottom line is that even if veiled and indistinct, the boys saw a world beyond Creston Avenue that they had the potential to join if they tried. They witnessed in concrete fashion the relevance of education to their futures.

• *They were acquainted with higher education.* Juan Carlos decided to apply to college after visiting Vassar, and Carlos made the same decision after spending time on campus with Juan Carlos. In short, despite fears about how they would fit in on campus, the boys no longer viewed college as wholly alien or as something reserved for people unlike themselves, which is the experience for many poor, urban youngsters of color, who know little or nothing about college.

• *They found the right college.* For Juan Carlos and Carlos, this translated into adequate financial aid, caring admissions counselors, a transition program, and a good fit socially and academically. Each of these ingredients is essential. In the end, the fit was not perfect, and Juan Carlos came home and transferred to a New York City college, but this had as much to do with circumstances in his life as with a bad academic fit.

Recall that Lisandro, Leo's brother, was accepted and planned to attend Johnson and Wales College, but learned that his financial package was insufficient to cover the costs and withdrew. He was able to attend a public college in New York the following year with the financial support of the HEOP program.

For low-income youngsters, the cost of college is not only a barrier, but few understand the difference between the sticker price and the actual cost of attending, which is frightening because the sticker price is frequently more than their parents earn annually. They generally know little about the multiplicity of financial aid programs that may be available to them. When they do learn something about them, the combination of federal, state, local, private and institutional possibilities are bewildering, and the paperwork and bureaucracy associated with them can be overwhelming. Low-income youngsters are also likely to need loans for tens of thousands of dollars. And institutions of higher education have increased the proportion of financial aid being awarded on the basis of merit rather than student need, which may improve institutional rankings in the *U.S. News and World Report* ratings, but reduces access to college by low-income and middle-class students.

One of the reasons Carlos applied, was accepted, and matriculated at Mount Saint Mary College was because of its committed and caring HEOP counselors. They did three things for him—encouraged Carlos to apply and helped him with the process, rigorously assessed his suitability for the program and for the college, and were persistent, once they accepted Carlos, in clearing the paperwork hurdles that stood in the way, calling and writing again and again while he was in the Dominican Republic during the summer. They need not have done this because they had a long wait list to take Carlos's place and many had higher grades and test scores than Carlos. They believed in him and extended him every opportunity to succeed.

Similarly, when Juan Carlos visited the HEOP office after his first few weeks at the college, and told the director he was going to quit because he just didn't fit and missed the old neighborhood, the director convinced him to give it another chance.

The HEOP transition program included the key elements students coming from isolated, low-income communities need if they are to have a chance to bridge the gap between the Creston Avenues from which they come and the hallowed ivy halls to which they are moving. Juan Carlos and Carlos received academic instruction designed to strengthen their basic skills and to prepare them for the rigors and expectations of college classes.

They learned about the social aspects of college and living in a largely white, far more affluent community. In Arthur's study with Jana Nidiffer, low-income students of color often told him about the enormous sense of loneliness and difference they felt on campus. They said they did not know their classmates' music, did not understand their humor, and did not comprehend their fashions.

The transition program explored the affective and personal aspects of college life. The HEOP students would be caught between two worlds. They were different from their classmates and would become increasingly different from the friends and relatives they left at home. Working in the program were people who had been through HEOP and could help the new students understand what lay ahead and how to cope. One advised Juan Carlos to run for class president.

While overwhelmingly White and middle class, Mount Saint Mary's also had a very small but critical mass of low-income Latinos to support one another. The college was small enough in size for students not to get lost, to get to know each other, and to be able to participate in campus activities with little fear of getting cut or dismissed. It was the kind of place where Juan Carlos could run for and be elected class president. The downside for students who felt they were different is that the college's smallness made it feel claustrophobic, magnifying their differences, particularly race. The college also offered academic and counseling services to HEOP students and had the advantage that Arthur enjoyed at Brandeis. It was a Catholic college. Both Juan Carlos and Carlos were Catholic as well.

These ingredients—mentors, experience with college and life beyond Creston Avenue, obtaining counseling and financial aid, and finding the right college with a transition program—were critical in getting Carlos and Juan Carlos to college, in helping them beat the odds. Had other elements been present, the road would likely have been smoother and less bumpy.

*   *   *

While the HEOP program had real strengths, parent education about college was missing. Carlos's dad wanted desperately for his son to succeed, but he lacked the knowledge and mechanics of how to accomplish this in the United States. It would have made an enormous difference to offer him a Spanish language program that could have helped Ismael better understand the labor market in the United States—the most promising fields for Carlos to study, the salaries associated with different careers, and the levels of education necessary to enter them. It would have been useful for Ismael to learn about how New York City public schools work with regard to essential subjects for his son to study, homework, tests, grades, report cards, text books and other learning materials, attendance, and academic progress. It would have been helpful for Ismael to learn about the importance of college, requirements for admission, different types of institutions, costs, financial aid, and collegiate study. It would have been valuable for Ismael to know how to be an advocate for his son in choosing schools, assessing their quality, and addressing problems encountered along the way. It would have been wonderful for Ismael to meet Dominican youngsters who succeeded and could serve as models for him of what Carlos might be able to achieve. But no such program existed.

Carlos and Juan Carlos came to the Bronx when they were already enrolled in school, but ideally, parent support programs should begin in the prenatal period, when future fathers and mothers can learn about parenting—nutrition, medical checkups, discipline, informal education, the importance of talking and reading to children, and all of the subjects essential for children to be ready for school and for life. Given the income status of parents, small honoraria would have been an excellent vehicle for attracting them and sustaining them through parenting programs.

On the flip side, teachers need a comparable intensive primer, and continuing education on the lives of their students and their families and the cultures from which they come; not only through lectures and readings, but through immersion into the communities in which they work. They need to study schools that are successful in educating students like their own and to understand why they are successful. They need to be able make schools welcoming environments for parents rather than places that intimidate and shame.

There were no early identification or intervention programs for Carlos and Juan Carlos either. When Jana and Arthur carried out their study, they asked the students who attended Harvard, when they knew they were special, having no idea what they meant by the question.[8] However, all but one of the students, without asking for clarification or further explanation, gave them an age or grade level. They learned early, like Arthur and his friends, that they were bound for college.

Juan Carlos and Carlos did not decide to go to college until their junior and senior year of high school. By that time, they had no idea about what they needed to study to be admitted, what grades were required, what their choices were, how they went about applying, how they would pay for college, or a million other things that middle-class children are taught long before. Juan Carlos was very lucky to have an excellent counselor, and Carlos was very fortunate to have Juan Carlos.

Hand in hand with early identification, Jana and Arthur found that college bound low-income students were often beneficiaries of intervention and enrichment activities. Arthur and Jana asked the Harvard students when they first thought about attending that university. The initial response was senior year of high school. When pressed, many remembered collegiate summer programs during their sophomore and junior years of high school. They recalled science fairs, debates, camps, trips, and academic competitions much earlier.

Those who attended high-achieving schools described years, beginning in elementary school, of being prepped for college, with information sessions for students and their parents, college visits and visits from colleges, guidance meetings, meet-the-alumni gatherings, test preparation, financial aid discussions, personal counseling, and much more. These are staples in schools where children are expected to go to college.

Four-year colleges and universities as a rule are not risk takers. Students don't attend higher education by accident. Enrichment and intervention activities are a vehicle for preparing low-income students for college. They are the acting equivalent of summer stock and regional theater.

The closest Juan Carlos came to such activities were his serendipitous Outward Bound experience, which proved life changing in discovering who he was and what he wanted to become, and his karate class, which while not academic, was a motivator in keeping him in school, providing him with a mentor, and teaching him about character and values. Carlos had no such experiences.

Neither boy had attended strong schools. Prior to Juan Carlos attending the Heritage School, they attended dangerous, overenrolled, underfunded schools which had low expectations for their students, faculty too often without expertise in the subjects they taught, poor teaching materials, weak curricula, dilapidated buildings, inadequate facilities, and low academic achievement by their students, who were not prepared for college. They were not expected to go to college. No child in America should have to attend such a school. They are relegated to such schools because of their race and income.

Arthur tells the story of a car crash he experienced after a snowstorm. His wife, Linda, and infant daughter, Jamie, were in the car. Up ahead, on the opposite side of the highway, was a pile-up of cars. Each had crashed into the one in front. Arthur witnessed another car smashing into the pile. He was angry with the driver for his inattention. He could have hit Arthur's car and hurt his family. A split second later, Arthur hit the same ice slick and began moving across four lanes of the highway into the crash site. The skid seemed to last for hours, not seconds. He slammed on the breaks, pumped them, hit the accelerator, steered left, steered right. All the while, Linda yelled at him: "Stop!" "Watch out!" "Jamie's in the car." She thought he was kidding, aping the latest crash victim. Linda didn't know he was out of control. He had no choice but to become part of the pile-up.

Every neighborhood has default tracks for its children's futures. In Arthur's case, the track took children to college and into the middle class. In Leo's, it led to lives of poverty, violence, discrimination, and bad schools. We call the track Arthur encountered the American Dream. We tend to shrug off Leo's track as the tragedy of our cities, too often casting blame on its victims.

In both cases, there are anomalies or exceptions: children like Juan Carlos and Carlos who make it, and children like Mark in Arthur's day who did not. They are boundary markers, who demonstrated the limits of the dream when Arthur grew up and today show the minimum requirements for extending the dream.

Extending
the American Dream

Leo's youngest niece: America's next generation

Today, Jarmaine Ollivierre is an aerospace engineer at NASA, and a cum laude graduate from Tuskegee University with a dual bachelor's degree in physics and aeronautical engineering. He also has a master's degree from Embry-Riddle Aeronautical University in Florida.

But in the fifth grade, he was a special education student living in a West Philadelphia neighborhood where the high school graduation rate for the class prior to his was only 26 percent. Jarmaine's mother, Patricia, the bedrock of his life, and, in his own words, the source of his motivation, was a single parent who worked two jobs to support her three children. . . . He credits his accomplishments to the decision by George Weiss to say "YES" to his education.

Say Yes to Education Web site

THIS CLOSING CHAPTER highlights three organizations that are at-tempting to extend the American dream to our nation's poorest children. They are translating the lessons of the anomalies on a grand scale, focusing on whole classes, schools, communities, and cit-ies. The oldest of the three is "I Have a Dream." The other two are the highly focused and ambitious "Harlem Children's Zone" and "Say Yes to Education" programs. Together these organizations demonstrate the very real possibility of making the American dream a reality for all of the nation's children and identify the direction public policy must take to achieve this.

I HAVE A DREAM

In 1981 Eugene Lang, a businessman and philanthropist, was asked to give the commencement address at the East Harlem elementary school he attended a half century before.[1] Lang planned to tell the students what speakers traditionally say in graduation speeches: "Work hard and you will succeed." That is, until the principal told him three-quarters of the students would probably never graduate from high school. Lang spontaneously changed his speech at the po-dium and "I Have a Dream" was born. He promised to pay the college tuition for all 61 sixth graders graduating that day if they completed high school.

Lang told the students about being on the Capitol Mall to hear Martin Luther King's "I Have a Dream" speech. He challenged them to dream their own dreams and promised to help them achieve those ambitions. Lang named his program after the speech and called the participants "Dreamers." But he quickly learned that the promise of a scholarship was insufficient to get the students to college. They were far behind academically and faced a raft of social and personal chal-lenges that served as profound barriers to high school graduation. Lang, while maintaining a close relationship with the kids, hired a full-time director for the program and provided the extensive supports and ser-vices necessary for his students to realize the Dream.

Four years later, all of Lang's Dreamers were still in school and his program was receiving extensive media coverage, including a front-page story in *The New York Times* and a segment on *60 Minutes*. Lang was barraged with inquiries from people who wanted to create their own "I Have a Dream" programs. In order to assist them, in 1986 he established the I Have a Dream Foundation, an umbrella organization providing assistance and support to sponsors, who funded their own programs.

In the years since, nearly 200 I Have a Dream programs have been spawned in 27 states, the District of Columbia, and New Zealand, serving more than 15,000 youngsters. The programs today are not only rooted in schools, but also housing projects and communities. The sponsors have been individuals, groups, not-for-profits and businesses. They have tended to identify children even earlier than Lang. Because the programs are individually sponsored, there has been significant variation in their quality and satisfaction of the sponsors. The Arete Corporation carried out an evaluation of the I Have a Dream program in eight local sites in 2001.[2] The research is now dated and based on studies using very different methodologies; however, the results demonstrate that "Dreamers" perform better academically, and graduate from high school and attend college at higher rates than peers. Among the Arete findings were the following:

In terms of academic performance, three studies found that Dreamers had significantly higher test scores and/or grades than their peers. For instance, in Portland Oregon, the proportion of eighth grade Dreamers meeting reading standards was 20% higher than control groups and in math twice as many Dreamers achieved the standard. A higher percentage of Dreamers also had grade point averages of C+ or better.

In terms of graduation rates, six studies found significantly higher secondary school completion rates for Dreamers than peers as judged by district averages or control groups. In 1993 and 1994 Chicago studies, 69% of Dreamers graduated versus 40% of their peers. Two years later, graduation rates rose to 75%, which was more than twice the rate of the district. Studies in Portland, Oregon and Patterson, New Jersey also demonstrated higher graduation rates, but by significantly smaller margins than in Chicago.

In terms of college attendance, four studies found significantly higher postsecondary enrollment rates for Dreamers than peers. In the 1996 Chicago study, which showed the most dramatic differences, Dreamers attended college at three times the rate of their classmates. Of Lang's initial sixth graders, 54 stayed in touch with the Foundation, and more than nine out of ten of them earned a high school diploma or equivalent (over three times the rate of their peers).[3] Six out of ten went on to some form of postsecondary education, attending institutions ranging across the public and private sectors, selective and nonselective schools, two and four year colleges.

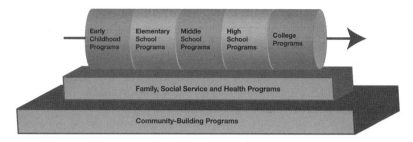

FIGURE 15.1. The HCZ Pipeline. (Used with permission of the Harlem Children's Zone.)

THE HARLEM CHILDREN'S ZONE

The Harlem Children's Zone® (HCZ®), led by Geoffrey Canada, is a more focused and centralized initiative, targeting one hundred blocks in central Harlem, an African-American community with a childhood poverty rate comparable to Arthur's old neighborhood. It is an ambitious project, which began with a single block in the late 1990's and now covers an area two to three times as large as Arthur's old neighborhood. Its goals are equally bold:

> to create a "tipping point" in the neighborhood so that children are surrounded by an enriching environment of college-oriented peers and supportive adults, a counterweight to "the street" and "a toxic popular culture that glorifies misogyny and anti-social behavior.[4]

To accomplish this, HCZ offers a comprehensive array of interrelated educational, social-service and community building initiatives and programs, prenatal through college graduation, targeted at children, parents, and community. HCZ depicts its pipeline of programs shown in Figure 15.1.[5] The program is built on five core principles:

- "Serve an entire neighborhood comprehensively and at scale" with the goals of reaching a great enough number of children to change the culture of the community, to improve the social and physical environment of the neighborhood that affects child development and to operate at a scale sufficient to meet community needs.
- "Create a pipeline of support" consisting of accessible, integrated, high quality programs aimed at young people,

families and the community that provide continuous scaffolding for the healthy development of children beginning with pre-natal programs and continuing through college graduation.

• "Build community among residents, institutions, and stakeholders" in order to foster, "the environment necessary for children's healthy development"

• "Evaluate program outcomes and create a feedback loop" to enable program refinement and improvement.

• "Cultivate a culture of success rooted in passion, accountability, leadership, and teamwork."

HCZ believes that its programs need to reach at least 65% percent of the children living in the target area to achieve a tipping point. Current costs run around $3500 per participant (adults and children) or $5,000 per child annually. Two-thirds of HCZ's funding comes from the philanthropic community. It has taken the Harlem Children's Zone 10 years to build the full HCZ Pipeline from birth through college graduation. Its programs seek to

(1) maximize educational achievements for poor children; (2) ensure that each of the programs in the pipeline is strong and incorporates best practices; (3) foster strong links across programs to smooth transitions and guarantee that programs are pedagogically continuous; (4) stay community-based and responsive to local community needs; and (5) provide relevant data to program staff so that they can improve services and to policymakers and decision makers so that they can get the best results on their investments.[6]

The HCZ effort translates into two schools, called the Promise Academy Charter Schools, the first of which opened in 2004.[7] As of 2008, they offer instruction from PreK to high school with the goal of giving neighborhood kids a rigorous, well-rounded and high quality education. They offer extended day and year round instruction, fresh meals, after-school programs ranging from academic support to electives such as web design, chess and photography and Saturday classes for students needing basic skills support. Admission is by lottery and the number of applicants far exceeds the enrollment capacity of the schools. Buttressing the schools are early childhood programs for all kinds of parents—expectant parents, parents with 3-year-olds, and all-day pre-kindergartens for children.

There are also programs tied to children's developmental levels, which seek to supplement the work of the schools. An elementary school initiative provides training in how to make the neighborhood safe for children and families. Middle school programs focus on health and fitness as well as academically assisting neighborhood children not enrolled at the Promise Academies. High school initiatives deal with the arts and media in addition to working with juniors and seniors on basic skills mastery and preparation for postsecondary education and the job market. A technology center teaches computer and job related skills to young people and adults. The College Success Office supports students who have graduated from high school in dealing with all aspects of higher education from access to graduation.

In addition, there are community and health initiatives. The Beacon programs turn school buildings into community centers for children and adults, offering afternoon, evening, weekend and summer academic and recreation programs. There are also programs for community organizing, asthma management, and obesity control. A health clinic was added to the Promise Academies in 2006 to provide students with free medical, dental and mental health services. A host of social services are offered too, including counseling, financial and legal consultation at several locations each week.

The motto of HCZ is "whatever works." Its programs are assessed regularly. Over time, they may be changed, dropped or replaced depending upon what works in achieving HCZ's goals. Some elements have been around for more than 35 years and others are recently created.

As would be expected, given the youth and evolving character of the HCZ initiative, the data on results are fragmentary. HCZ involved 10,883 young people in 2008, which is an impressive number, putting HCZ well on its path to a 65% participation rate. There is compelling evidence that the parents program is promoting increased reading to children and changes in discipline practices. The pre-school programs have a notable record in promoting school-readiness for their students. The results at the Promise Academies are also noteworthy. At Promise Academy 2, in 2008 all of the third-graders were at or above grade level on the 2008 state-wide math test. At Promise Academy 1, 97% of the third-graders performed comparably.

At Promise Academy 1 middle school, which enrolled a student body in sixth grade that tested 2 and 3 years behind grade level, the results have been impressive. By eighth grade 87% of the students scored at or above grade level on the New York State math exam.

SAY YES TO EDUCATION

Say Yes to Education is perhaps the most comprehensive of the programs. Created and funded by investor George Weiss, Say Yes seeks to increase high school and college graduation rates for inner-city young-sters. Reminiscent of I Have a Dream, Say Yes began in 1987 when Weiss promised a group of 112 Philadelphia sixth graders that if they completed high school, he would pay to send them to college.[8] Today, there are Say Yes programs in Philadelphia, Cambridge, Harlem, and Hartford.

Say Yes begins with the belief that disadvantaged children face four obstacles in getting to college—academic, socioemotional, financial, and health—and targets its programs at alleviating the obstacles.

Academically, the program is now rooted in early intervention. For instance, in New York City, Say Yes invited all of the children entering Kindergarten in five schools to participate in the program. The children undergo diagnostic assessments to identify strengths and weaknesses in order to provide appropriate supports and services. Students receive tutoring in areas of need, enrichment activities, and after-school and summer programs, including basic skills and literacy instruction as well as recreational and cultural activities. Say Yes provides support for parental involvement in education and professional development for teachers, and joins participating school leadership teams.

Socioemotionally, Say Yes builds relationships with the participating families, providing professional counselling, educational guidance, interventions, mentoring, legal counsel, and conflict resolution, as well as support groups for youngsters with prosocial peers.

Financially, Say Yes provides scholarships for students, parents, and siblings to attend postsecondary educational institutions.

With regard to health, Say Yes, through partnering hospitals and health care providers, offers medical, dental, and mental health services.

The Say Yes model has evolved over time with testing and evaluation to focus more on early intervention and work with families and their communities, accenting reading and literacy instruction, extending study time to include after-school and summer programs, and buttressing enrichment activities.

Say Yes is the smallest of the three programs. To date, 314 youngsters have completed the program, and 418 are currently in the pipeline.

The results are impressive. Say Yes participants do dramatically better than their peers. Seventy-six percent received high school diplomas or GED's. Fifty percent attended postsecondary education, and 26% received baccalaureate or higher degrees. Graduates have attended Ivy League universities, top research universities and liberal arts colleges, regional universities and colleges, Black colleges, community colleges, and technical schools.

Say Yes is currently launching its most ambitious program and perhaps the largest scale-up effort of this type ever undertaken—a whole city. Say Yes, Syracuse University, and the Syracuse City School District have formed a partnership to develop and implement the Syracuse Say Yes to Education and Economic Development Demonstration Program. In its first districtwide program, Say Yes will attempt to dramatically increase both high school and college graduation rates in an entire city.

At the core of the program will be the same elements that have characterized Say Yes since its earliest days—a promise to pay the cost of college, combined with a comprehensive support program, rooted in the barriers to college that poor kids face, and that begin when students enter kindergarten and continue until they graduate from high school.

All Syracuse City School District students are eligible to participate in the program, and 22 private colleges and universities and 70 State University and City University of New York public institutions have made commitments to provide them with free college tuition. Beyond the universities, Say Yes, and the school district, partners include the Syracuse city government, the state of New York, and the local business community.

CONCLUSION

Say Yes, the Harlem Children's Zone, and I Have a Dream demonstrate that the American Dream can be restored for youngsters in classes, public housing projects, schools, and communities. The programs share some important characteristics in how they accomplish this:

- *The program goals are explicit.* Each of the programs has the explicit and measurable goal of increasing high school and college graduation rates for disadvantaged children.
- *The programs are comprehensive.* They identify the obstacles children face to achieving their goals, and develop a suite of initiatives to combat them. In each case, these include the full range of activities that made it possible for Juan Carlos and Carlos to get to college, as well as those that were missing. Only HCZ was able to create new, high quality schools. Say Yes worked with the existing schools to improve performance.

- *The programs are both targeted and individualized.* They are targeted at specific classes, schools, and communities. Both Say Yes and the Harlem Children's Zone are seeking to build a critical mass of students in their programs, with the aim of changing the culture. In the words of George Weiss, this means transforming the road to college from a narrow potholed path for poor kids to a superhighway.

   However, the content of the programs are individualized to meet the needs of each child and family. The philosophy is not one size fits all, but rather one arm around one child. The educators involved in the programs are parents, teachers, counselors, peers, and other professionals. Each program seeks to form a personal relationship with participants and families. I Have a Dream and Say Yes attempt to build a personal bond between the participants and the sponsor.

- *The programs prepare mentors.* Say Yes and HCZ specifically identify the key people in a child's life at particular developmental stages and attempt to prepare them to serve as mentors. The underlying philosophy is that anyone with a significant role in a child's life has the potential to serve as a mentor and everyone in the child's life should have the skills and knowledge to do so.

- *The programs engage in early intervention.* I Have a Dream and Say Yes began with sixth graders, and each subsequently chose to focus on younger children in order to involve them before their academic shortcomings mounted further and their alienation from school grew larger. The Harlem Children's Zone had the earliest intervention strategy with its prenatal programs. The stories of Juan Carlos and Carlos demonstrate the precariousness of late intervention. For both, completing college has been fragile.

- *The programs offer students enrichment activities.* In order to assist youngsters limited by schools that operate 180 days a year from 8 a.m. to 3 p.m., each of the programs in varying degree added tutoring, counseling, after-school programs, and summer initiatives ranging across academic, cultural and entertainment activities, which are traditionally available to more affluent children. These were sparse in Juan Carlos's and Carlos's journey to college.

- *The programs give students guidance, assistance and support to attend college, to make the transition from the neighborhood to college, and to complete college.* These are the things Juan Carlos and Carlos were lucky to find in their most rudimentary forms. The students in Say Yes, HCZ, and I Have a Dream are treated to the deluxe versions—rich in content, frequent in communication, provided by experts, and begun early. They are guaranteed college tuition if they complete high school in I Have a Dream, and so are their parents and siblings in Say Yes. But there is a gap between aspirations and the realities of the programs. While the numbers of students completing postsecondary education are far higher in I Have a Dream and Say Yes than for peers, retention and graduation remain challenges in both programs.

- *The programs build coalitions of stakeholders.* The best examples of this are the Say Yes Syracuse program and the Harlem Children's Zone, which incorporated the individuals and organizations with the greatest capacity to embrace and sustain their programs. Coalitions increase the likelihood of program ownership, participation, support, and continuity when key stakeholders depart, as inevitably occurs in any long-term initiative. A coalition also offers the potential to help shape a program to meet the needs of a specific community, to aid the program in avoiding local potholes, and to protect it against unwarranted criticism.

- *The programs are committed to evidence-based third-party assessment.* Such evaluation is occurring in varying degree in all three programs. This is essential because the typical educational initiative is declared a success based upon anecdotes and satisfaction surveys. We need evidence based research so we know what works.

- *The programs are funded largely with private dollars.* Geoffrey Canada believes this is essential to avoid the politicization that comes with government leadership. Instead, he favors partnerships with government support, but not control.

- *The programs are demonstration sites.* Each is attempting to achieve similar goals but is going about it in different ways. This makes the three programs excellent labs for studying how to improve educational attainment in low-income communities and developing policy to scale-up best practice.

- *None of the programs seeks to transform the local public schools.* After a 25-year school-reform movement, not one major urban school district in this country has been successfully turned around. Recognizing this, I Have a Dream worked around the local schools. Say Yes attempted improvements in the participating schools via professional development and joining school leadership teams. The Harlem

Children's Zone superseded the local schools with charters. The simple fact is that even for three bold and innovative programs, the challenge of transforming failing schools into high-quality institutions was too daunting to undertake.

There appear to be three avenues of redress in this area. The first is the courts. There are a growing number of educational adequacy suits, asserting that a quality education is a civil right, and systematic differences in educational outcomes are the result of educational inequalities. A majority of these cases are being won by the plaintiffs. The second approach is to do what the Harlem Children's Zone did, replace the existing schools with charters. And the third is to organize communities again, as HCZ is doing. Parents may need to take to the streets to demonstrate against failing schools. If these schools are not good enough for wealthier kids, they are not good enough for their kids. They may need to tell politicians their vote will be reserved exclusively for candidates who will improve their schools.

The most important commonality in the three programs is that they demonstrate that America has the capacity today to reduce the number of children lost unnecessarily like Leo, and to dramatically increase the proportion, like Juan Carlos and Carlos, who are graduating from high school and attending college. We, as a nation, can restore the American Dream for all of our children.

We know what it takes to raise high school and postsecondary graduation rates. We know why Juan Carlos, Carlos, and the other anomalies did not succumb to the neighborhood. We have important experiments and demonstrations on how to accomplish this at varying scale and scalability in the Harlem Children's Zone, I Have a Dream, and Say Yes to Education. They offer the promise of answering some essential questions:

- When is intervention most effective?
- How effective are various types of interventions?
- What are the costs of effective intervention?
- How should interventions be funded?
- Is effective intervention sustainable?
- How can effective intervention be brought to scale?
- How can effective interventions be translated into policy with the capacity to save all of our children?

As a nation, we need to save our children because it makes financial sense. Study after study shows that the amount of money spent as a consequence of poverty in health care costs, welfare, crime, courts, prisons, and social services is far greater than the costs of programs like I Have a Dream, the Harlem Children's Zone, and Say Yes to Education. The real choice facing us today is whether we want to invest in our children when they are young and promising or wait to pay for them when they are older and broken.

Our orientation in writing this book is pragmatic. We are losing children every day. They can't wait for ideal or long-term, systematic solutions. In offering proposals for action, we ask the *Schindler's List* question: How many can be saved right now?

Accordingly, we have chosen to focus on overcoming the immediate barriers to social mobility for poor children rather than the systemic causes of poverty, though it is imperative that the nation grapple with these issues as well. We emphasize sure things over long shots. We are more concerned with what is possible today, rather than more far-reaching but speculative long-term remedies. We favor scaling up existing programs with strong track records that serve thousands of children instead of developing comprehensive policy agendas that might someday reach millions of children—though we believe this too is needed, it should grow out of the successful practice of existing programs. We focus on education as the primary path out of poverty rather than embracing more comprehensive remedies to the ills that undermine it, including inadequate housing, jobs, and healthcare.

We recognize the limitations in our approach. What we are proposing is a kind of triage: patching broken institutions, supplementing failing schools, and creating laboratories or innovative enclaves within the existing infrastructure. The future requires more: focusing on causes rather than symptoms, embracing not only education but all of the realities that serve as barriers to mobility, and adopting nationally the policies and programs that will make the American dream universally available to our children.

We have an obligation to save our children. Because we are a good and decent people, we know that it is immoral to deny children a future because they were born poor or have the "wrong" skin color. We must also save them because we have to. Our democracy and our economy require an educated citizenry. America cannot thrive as a permanently divided nation of haves and have nots.

Epilogue:
Where Are They Now?

Miriam—Leo's mom lives in the Bronx in the same apartment where we met her almost 10 years ago and works full-time earning just above minimum wage as a home attendant caring for elderly adults. She lives with her brother Siso and cousin Gustavo, who both work in construction. Miriam was finally able to complete her house in the Dominican Republic. A year later, two men entered the house, held up her brother Radhame at gun and knife point, and stole everything.

Lisandro—Leo's brother, Lisandro, broke up with Betty and moved out of her house within 2 years of their daughter's birth. He tried to go back to college, but because he had previously received financial aid for college and did not finish, he was not allowed to get additional financial support until he paid back his prior school debt. Lisandro is living in Texas working with cars. His daughter and ex-girlfriend, Betty, live in New York City. He has not returned to college.

Moreno—Leo's dad, Moreno, is living in the Bronx. Moreno and Miriam are now friends.

Maholi—Leo's sister, Maholi, lives in Brooklyn with her high school boyfriend and baby daughter, born in 2008. She works at her boyfriend's family-run day-care center in East New York, Brooklyn. She didn't graduate from high school. Maholi and Miriam made peace over the stolen money, and Maholi's daughter is the shining star in her grandma's life.

Ana—Leo's former girlfriend, Ana, has a baby daughter. She lived briefly in North Carolina, where she worked in housekeeping/maintenance at JCPenney. In 2009 she moved back to New York City and temporarily lived in a homeless shelter while looking for an apartment. Ana has not completed her GED.

Juan Carlos—Juan Carlos currently works full-time in the president's office at Teachers College as an administrative assistant. He is a semester shy of graduating from Baruch College in political science and plans to attend graduate school. He lives in a one-bedroom apartment in the South Bronx with his girlfriend Jakiris and 1-year-old son, Jariel.

Carlos—Carlos is a term away from graduation at Mount Saint Mary College with a major in Human Services and a concentration in Criminal Justice. His girlfriend, Venus, gave birth to their baby girl, Destiny, in the summer of 2009. He lives with his girlfriend's family and his daughter in the South Bronx.

Aneudys—Leo's friend Aneudys moved to Atlanta. He was enrolled in a medical assistant program, but did not complete it. After living briefly in Texas with Lisandro he moved back to New York, and is working at a clothing store. He would like to go back to school and study film, but because he has outstanding student loans, he cannot get the necessary financial aid to return to school. His girlfriend is due to give birth in May, 2010.

Jim—Arthur's friend Jim retired as a school principal and his wife, Rhonda, as a teacher, and they moved to Florida.

Barry—Arthur's friend Barry and his wife, Susan, both retired as teachers and are living in New Jersey.

Debby—Arthur's friend Debby is working as a nurse in Troy, New York. Her husband, Art, has retired as a union organizer, and Debby is now the proud grandmother to a baby girl.

The memorial to Leo on the corner of Creston and Burnside Avenues remains.

The big red gate that barred the front of Arthur and Carlos's building is no longer there—perhaps a sign of hope of a safer neighborhood.

Notes

Acknowledgments

1. The names of several people in this volume have been changed at their request. Even in these acknowledgments, we use those pseudonyms. But they know who they are and how very grateful we are to them.

Prologue

1. They were paid minimum wage for the time spent keeping the diaries, both as a vechicle to ensure they gave adequate time and attention to their writing and as compensation for wages forgone.

Chapter 5

1. See New York City Department of City Planning (2009).
2. See Smith (2008).
3. See U.S. Department of Education (2002).

Chapter 7

1. A lot of the expensive name-brand clothes that Leo wore belonged to his brother, Lisandro. Lisandro made money at his grocery store job and by participating in pharmaceutical studies, where he once earned $5,000. Leo earned an hourly minimum wage anytime he worked on this research project. His mom also gave him money when she could.

Chapter 8

1. Leo used the minimum hourly wage he received for working on this research project to pay Ana's rent.

Chapter 13

1. Laura served as convener and recorder at all of the meetings and post-meeting debriefings.

2. Earlier in this book statistics were cited from the 2000 U.S. Census to set the stage for Leo's story. Note that in this discussion data are updated to 2007 and refer to the Congressional District rather than the smaller neighborhood census tract. See U.S. Census Bureau (2008a, b, c, d).

3. The salary and poverty threshold are for the year 2002 when Leo, Lisandro, and Maholi still lived at home. See U.S. Census Bureau (2002).

4. See U.S. Department of Labor (2008).

5. See U.S. Census Bureau (2008b, c, d), and U.S. Department of Education (2008a).

6. See Levitt and Dubner (2009).

7. See U.S. Census Bureau (2008b, c, d).

8. Since Leo attended elementary school, the gap in average teacher salaries between NYC urban and suburban schools has decreased. This is partly due to the substantial increase in NYC teacher supporting salaries (a 43% increase as of 2002, according to the NYC Department of Education). In 2008, the average starting salary ranged from $45,530 to $74,796, depending on training and years of experience. See New York City Department of Education (2009).

9. Juan Carlos, as will be discussed later, did attend the Heritage high school, an excellent school, and learned how poor the schools he and his friends were forced to attend actually were. With that realization came the more than justified anger.

Chapter 14

1. See U.S. Department of Education (2008b).
2. See U.S. Department of Education (2008a).
3. U.S. Department of Education (2008b).
4. See Haveman and Smeeding (2006).
5. U.S. Department of Education (2008b).
6. Haveman and Smeeding (2006).
7. See Levine and Nidiffer (1996).
8. Ibid.

Chapter 15

1. See the I Have a Dream Foundation (n.d.) Web site (http://www.ihavead-reamfoundation.org).

2. See Arete Corporation (2001).

3. The I Have a Dream (n.d.) Web site (http://www.ihaveadreamfoundation.org).

4. See the Harlem Children Zone's Web site (http://www.hcz.org).

5. See the Harlem Children Zone's Project Model Exedutive Summary (n.d.).

6. Ibid.

7. See the Harlem Children's Zone Web site (http://www.hcz.org).

8. See the Say Yes to Education Web site (http://www.sayyestoeducation.org/site/index.php).

Bibliography

Arete Corporation. (2001). *I have a dream: The impacts.* Retrieved December 20, 2009, from http://www.ihaveadreamfoundation.org/images/downloads/AreteSummary_2003.pdf

Berliner, D. (2004). Describing the behavior and documenting the accomplishments of expert teachers. *Bulletin of Science, Technology & Society, 24*(3), 200–212.

Brennan, J. F. (n.d.). *New York City public school student improvement before and after mayoral control.* Retrieved December 18, 2009 from http://assembly.state.ny.us/member_files/044/20090128/report.pdf

Day, C. (1999). *Developing teachers: The challenges of lifelong learning* (Educational Change and Development Series). Bristol: Taylor & Francis.

Gootman, E. (2003, October14). Lunch at 9:21, and students are the sardines. *The New York Times,* p. B6. Retrieved December 20, 2009, from http://www.nytimes.com/2003/10/14/nyregion/lunch-at-9-21-and-students-are-the-sardines.html

Haggerty, R. A. (Ed.) (1991). *Dominican Republic and Haiti: Country studies* (Area Handbook Series, 2nd ed.). Washington, DC: United States Government Printing Office.

The Harlem Children's Zone Project Model Executive Summary. (n.d.). Retrieved December 18, 2009, from http://www.tc.edu/i/a/document/9857_ExecutiveSummaryHCZ09.pdf

The Harlem Children's Zone (HCZ) (2009, December 7). Retrieved December 18, 2009, from http://www.hcz.org/

Haveman, R., & Smeeding, T. (2006). The role of higher education in social mobility. *Opportunity in America,*16(2).

I Have a Dream. (n.d.). *About us, history.* Retrieved December 18, 2009, from http://www.ihaveadreamfoundation.org/html/history.htm

I Have a Dream. (n.d.). *About us, impact.* Retrieved December 18, 2009, from http://www.ihaveadreamfoundation.org/html/impact.htm

Jones, J. (2002). *South Bronx rising: The rise, fall, and resurrection of an American city.* Bronx: Fordham University Press.

Kozol, J. (1992). *Savage inequalities: Children in America's schools.* New York: Harper Perennial.

Levine, A., & Nidiffer, J. (1996). *Beating the odds: How the poor get to college.* San Francisco: Jossey-Bass.

Levitt, S. D., & Dubner, S.J. (2009). *Freakonomics: A rogue economist explores the hidden side of everything.* New York: Harper Perennial.

New York City Department of City Planning. (2009a). *New York City census factfinder, 2000 Census profiles for New York City, census tracts, Bronx 235.01, demographic profile.* Retrieved from December 19, 2009, from http://gis.nyc.gov/dcp/pa/Map?hseNumber=2078&address=Creston+Avenue&borough=2&event=PROCESS_TRACT&sltdMBuffer=0.25&entry=1&smind=SINGLE

New York City Department of City Planning. (2009b). *New York City census factfinder, 2000 census profiles for New York City, census tracts, Bronx 235.02, demographic profile.* Retrieved from December 19, 2009, from http://gis.nyc.gov/dcp/pa/Map?mapWindow.x=291&mapWindow.y=192&mapaction=SINGLE&layer=nyct2000&stats=Demographic&sx=0&sy=0&boro=2&dir=&event=SINGLE&entry=5&sltdMBuffer=

New York City Department of City Planning. (2009c). *New York City census factfinder, 2000 census profiles for New York City, census tracts, Bronx 235.01, Socioeconomic profile.* Retrieved from December 19, 2009, http://gis.nyc.gov/dcp/pa/Map?mapWindow.x=266&mapWindow.y=160&mapaction=SINGLE&layer=nyct2000&stats=General&sx=0&sy=0&boro=2&dir=&event=SINGLE&entry=5&sltdMBuffer=

New York City Department of City Planning. (2009d). *New York City census factfinder, 2000 census profiles for New York City, census tracts, Bronx 235.02, Socioeconomic profile.* Retrieved from December 19, 2009, http://gis.nyc.gov/dcp/pa/Map?mapaction=SINGLE&layer=nyct2000&stats=General&sx=0&sy=563&boro=2&dir=&event=NEW_STATS&entry=5&sltdMBuffer=

New York City Department of Education. (2009). *Salary.* Retrieved December 15, 2009, from http://schools.nyc.gov/TeachNYC/SalaryBenefits/Salary/default.html

New York State Education Department. (2008). *New York state education department information, reporting and technology services salary percentiles for classroom teachers 2007–2008* (pp. 26–27). Retrieved November 10, 2009, from http://www.emsc.nysed.gov/irts/pmf/2007-08/2008_Stat-14.pdf

Rosenthal, M., Rosler, M., & Phillips, B. (2000). *In the South Bronx of America.* Willimantic: Curbstone Press.

Say Yes to Education. (n.d.-a). *Approach.* Retrieved December 19, 2009, from http://www.sayyestoeducation.org/syte/content/blogcategory/1/31/

Say Yes to Education. (n.d.-b). *Syracuse University.* Retrieved December 19, 2009, from http://www.sayyestoeducation.org/syte/content/blogcategory/18/32/

Say Yes to Education (n.d.-c). *Results.* Retrieved December 19, 2009, from http://www.sayyestoeducation.org/syte/content/blogcategory/19/33/

Say Yes to Education (n.d.-d). *Results.* Retrieved December 19, 2009, from http://www.sayyestoeducation.org/syte/content/view/47/63/

Smith, C. (2008). *Minimum wage history.* Retrieved November 1, 2009, from http://oregonstate.edu/instruct/anth484/minwage.html

Tough, P. (2008). *Whatever it takes: Geoffrey Canada's quest to change Harlem and America.* Boston: Houghton Mifflin.

Ultan L. & Unger, B. (2000). *Bronx accent. A literary and pictorial history of the borough.* New Brunswick: Rutgers University Press.

U.S. Bureau of the Census. (1961). *U.S. census of population 1960 U.S. summary.* Vol. 1, pt. 1 (p. I-207). Washington DC: U.S. Government Printing Office.

U.S. Bureau of the Census. (1962). *U.S. census of population and housing 1960. Census tracts final report PHC (1) -104, part 1.* Washington DC: US Government Printing Office.

U.S. Census Bureau. (2002). *Poverty thresholds.* Retrieved December 15, 2009, from http://www.census.gov/hhes/www/poverty/threshld/thresh02.html

U.S. Census Bureau. (2008a). *The American community survey.* Available from http://www.census.gov/acs/www/

U.S.CensusBureau.(2008b).Congressionaldistrict16,NewYork(110thcongress): ACSdemographicandhousingestimates:2007.RetrievedDecember20,2009, fromhttp://factfinder.census.gov/servlet/ADPTable?_bm=y&-zip=10453&- context=adp&-qr_name=ACS_2007_1YR_G00_DP5&-street=2078%20 Creston%20Avenue%20&-ds_name=&-city=Bronx%20&-tree_id=307&- redoLog=false&-all_geo_types=N&-geo_id=50000US3616&-format=&-_ lang=en&-states=New%20York

U.S. Census Bureau. (2008c). Congressional district 16, New York (110th congress): Selected Economic Characteristics: 2007. Retrieved from December 20,2009,fromhttp://factfinder.census.gov/servlet/ADPTable?_bm=y&-geo_ id=50000US3616&-qr_name=ACS_2007_1YR_G00_DP3&-ds_name=&-_ lang=en&-redoLog=false

U.S. Census Bureau. (2008d). *Congressional district 16, New York (110th Congress): Selected social characteristics in the United States: 2007.* Retrieved December 20, 2009, from http://factfinder.census.gov/servlet/ADPTable?_bm=y&-_geo_id=500$50000US3616:Y&-zip=10453&-context=adp&- qr_name=ACS_2007_1YR_G00_DP2&-street=2078%20Creston%20 Avenue%20&-ds_name=ACS_2007_1YR_G00_&-city=Bronx%20&-tree_ id=307&-_execClient=Y&-redoLog=false&-all_geo_types=N&-geo_ id=500$50000US3616&-_stateSelectedFromDropDown=New%20York&- format=&-_lang=en&-states=New%20York

U.S. Department of Education. (2002). National Center of Education Statistics. Available from http://nces.ed.gov/pubs2002/droppub2001/tables/tableA.asp

U.S. Department of Education. (2008a). National Center of Education Statistics. Available from http://nces.ed.gov/programs/digest/d08/tables/ ott08_110.asp

U.S. Department of Education. (2008b). Number of persons 18 and over by highest education attained by age, sex, and race/ethnicity. Percentage of high school dropouts among persons 16–24 years old (status drop out) by income level, percent distribution of status dropouts by labor force status and educational attainment: 1970–2007. *Digest of Educational Statistics.* (Tables 9–10).

U.S. Department of Labor. (2008). *Occupational employment projections to 2016* by Arlene Dohm & Lynn Shniper. Retrieved December 15, 2009, from. http://www.bls.gov/opub/mlr/2007/11/art5full.pdf

About the Authors

Arthur Levine is the President of the Woodrow Wilson National Fellowship Foundation and President Emeritus of Teachers College, Columbia University. In the past, he has also been a faculty member at the Harvard Graduate School of Education, President of Bradford College, and a senior fellow at the Carngie Council on Policy Studies in Higher Education and Carnegie Foundation for the Advancement of Teaching. He is a prolific author on issues of schools and colleges.

Laura Scheiber is a Ph.D. student in Comparative and International Education at Teachers College, Columbia University. A Fulbright grant recipient, her doctoral research focuses on innovative leaders of violence prevention and youth empowerment initiatives in Brazil. She earned a M.A. at Teachers College, specializing in international educational development and adult education, and earned a B.A. in psychology from Ohio University. In addition to being a former anchorperson for After Ed News, she has also taught college-level courses on child development and is a consultant on topics related to international transitions.